THIRTEEN WAVES

THIRTEEN WAVES

A REFLECTION ON CHALLENGES, FAILURES, AND LESSONS LEARNED

LEE D. BECK

HOUNDSTOOTH
PRESS

THIRTEEN WAVES

A Reflection on Challenges, Failures, and Lessons Learned

ISBN   978-1-5445-1638-7 *Hardcover*

978-1-5445-1637-0 *Paperback*

978-1-5445-1636-3 *Ebook*

Dear Cole, Will, and Jake,

Thank you for the inspiration to write this book. I hope you live your best lives and this helps you in some way. I love you and thank you for making my life better every day.

Dad

CONTENTS

"It is not the critic who counts; not the man who points out how the strong man stumbles, or where the doer of deeds could have done them better. The credit belongs to the man who is actually in the arena, whose face is marred by dust and sweat and blood; who strives valiantly; who errs, who comes short again and again, because there is no effort without error and shortcoming; but who does actually strive to do the deeds; who knows great enthusiasms, the great devotions; who spends himself in a worthy cause; who at the best knows in the end the triumph of high achievement, and who at the worst, if he fails, at least fails while daring greatly, so that his place shall never be with those cold and timid souls who neither know victory nor defeat."

—THEODORE ROOSEVELT, APRIL 23, 1910,
PARIS, FRANCE, "THE MAN IN THE ARENA"

INTRODUCTION

I believe society has lost its way in raising boys to be great men. We read every day of another school shooting, lack of diversity, fraternity hazing, bullying, domestic violence, suicide, and case after case of anxiety and depression. In all of these issues, men are disproportionately involved or affected.

When my boys were still young, their mother and I divorced, and I felt lost in many ways. Though I was fortunate to receive countless free and unsolicited recommendations from strangers and friends on how to raise boys, I never found a manual on how to raise good men, and I searched everywhere. I was able to find advice on everything from potty training, to disciplinary measures, to first aid, but not on how to build character or teach my boys the foundational lessons of life needed to grow into strong, caring, resilient men.

In my own life, I learned these lessons the hard way with tough but instructive experiences. I always knew I wanted to pass these lessons onto my sons. I thought about writing this book for years, but I kept putting it off. And then I was diagnosed with cancer.

Suddenly, I realized that I really didn't have all the time in the world. I began thinking about what mattered most and whether I had given my boys the lessons and insights that could help them be their best selves and live their best lives. That was the catalyst for taking the words in my head and finally putting them to paper.

In the months between my cancer diagnosis and surgery, I started this book, writing down the moments in my life that had taught me valuable lessons. I wanted to share my experiences and advice, not because I was perfect during my past, but because the lessons from my past had led to my growth. The cumulative effect of the challenges and failures provided me with great awareness of myself, which allowed me to develop a bridge for continuous discussion with my three sons, creating a space for safe, vulnerable, and respectful dialogue. I believe fostering awareness in a boy's soul allows him to better appreciate, accept, love, and respect himself more, allowing him to in turn better appreciate, accept, love, and respect strangers and loved ones alike.

I wrote this book for my three boys. I never planned nor expected anyone else would read it. I recall telling the publisher after they expressed interest that I would need only four copies printed, three for my sons and one for me so I could remember what I wrote. I don't think of myself as a writer, and I am still scared to think of people I know and don't know reading about my life and thinking how poor of a writer I am and how boring this book is. However, while I wrote this book with my sons in mind, I believe the larger lessons are applicable to everyone. My hope for this book—and for you—is that these words help to spark your own discussions about what it means to live the best version of yourself and your best life. I hope that by reading my experiences, you will be reminded of your own formative life lessons and be inspired to share them—without needing a cancer diagnosis to push you into action. Whether you are someone raising boys or you are a young man hoping to better connect with your parents or other guardian, if just one chapter or sentence serves as a cata-lyst for a thoughtful discussion, then this book is worth it. The gift in this book is awareness, that we are not alone, that we all have challenges, but that if we have the courage to ask questions and discuss our feelings, our lives will be more successful and fulfilling. As I learned long ago, life is not about possessions; it's about a collection of shared experiences. May this book give you a starting point from which to build shared experiences with your loved ones.

As you read through the book, each chapter contains a unique true story. I focused on challenging times and many failures, as they provided me the greatest insight to what I had done wrong, what I had overlooked or not considered, what I had underprepared for or quite simply not understood. Although I have many proud moments in my life that I would be happy to reflect upon, that's not what provided the greatest teaching. At the end of each story is a short letter to my sons summarizing a key awareness or lesson that I hope they reference when challenges occur in their life.

I don't have all the answers. This book is not a manual on what to do and how. I don't profess to be any smarter than anyone else attempting to solve life. I don't consider myself the perfect father or parent. I have made countless mistakes and will continue to do so (I actually hope I didn't screw my sons up too much!). I'm just trying to make a difference in how boys think and feel in an age when thinking and feeling should be prioritized instead of sequestered.

Before we get started, a quick note on the book's title. I titled the book based on an altercation I had with a coral reef and an unforeseen large set of waves in the Indian

Ocean during a trip a few years ago. I am no Kelly Slater nor would I say I'm a great surfer, but I love finding remote locations around the world and learning how much I still don't know. This particular experience occurred during a unique time in my life, and it resonated with the physical, intellectual, emotional, and spiritual peaks and valleys I have faced.

When you spend some time surfing, you learn that waves tend to come in sets, one after another before there's a break. Similarly, lessons in our life are often part of a set, building upon one another. In this book, I share thirteen lessons total, hence the title *Thirteen Waves*. (There's more significance to that number that you'll discover later.)

In surfing and in life, the waves will always come. How you handle them is up to you.

Now get ready for the first wave...

LESSON #1

BUILD RELATIONSHIPS ON CARE AND RESPECT, NOT FEAR

My brother, Jay, and I are sitting at the dinner table. I'm in fifth grade, which would put Jay in third. We're eating brussels sprouts with apple cider vinegar to bury the taste. Well, we're supposed to be eating them. We're not allowed to get up from the table until we're done, but boys and brussels sprouts rarely mix well. We're basically staring at the oddities, stuck there with nothing else to do, and two boys with nothing else to do goes south pretty quickly. We start giggling.

"Boys, you got to shut it down! Just quiet down," my dad calls, his voice carrying from the living room, where he is sitting in his tan recliner watching TV. It is the first warning.

We don't really pay attention to the first warning, and it is quickly followed by a second. "If you guys don't shut up, I'm going to crack your fucking heads together!" he shouts in a more serious voice. That's when the laughter bursts out. We were already riled up, and his yelling just seems funny.

Then the final warning comes, quieter but more impactful than the first two. My dad's recliner has a handle on the side to put the footrest up and down. Whenever he pulls it, it clicks, and the footrest snaps back into place.

Click. Snap. That is our final warning that he's not happy and is coming our way. That means it's go time.

Both of us take off in two different directions. It is pure survival at this point. We already know every angle and exit strategy in the house from previous nights. We're like bank robbers who studied the quickest routes out. I head toward the stairs, pretty sure I can beat Jay. While it may not be pretty, the truth is the one who gets out ahead initially has a better chance. And we both want to be ahead.

At the top of the stairs, I veer left into my room. I'm lucky because my bed is tucked into the corner. If I dive under and crawl far enough and fast enough into the back corner, my dad can't reach me. I can tighten up into a ball and don't have to worry. Whichever direction his arms come from, I can move just a little bit and stay out of the way. Eventually, he'll get frustrated and leave, often times to go find Jay. It doesn't feel like I've won anything.

My brother doesn't fare as well. His bed is in the middle of his room. When he goes underneath, my dad can move around the bed, as Jay shifts from side to side. My dad ultimately grabs his ankle and pulls him out from underneath. Sometimes, I think Jay has the worst of it for the simple reason of the bed location. If I'm not home, Jay goes straight for my room instead.

Once caught, we know what is coming. On the brussels sprouts night, I peer into Jay's room and see Jay hanging upside down with his ankles in my dad's left hand. My dad is big enough and strong enough that he can hold us like that in one hand and pull his belt off with his right hand. I can hear it coming through the loops. It's a sound I will never forget.

Have you ever had a firecracker go off right behind you when you didn't expect it? That's the physical reaction I had. It was a developed response. When my dad pulled his belt from his pants, it was as if someone dropped a firecracker. My body tightened up. Every single muscle shook. Thoughts would run through my head. *How do I get out of here? Where do I go?* Later, my stomach would be upset and my head would hurt. I didn't understand why at the time, but it was likely the adrenaline. And there was always the constant underlying question, "How do I get out of this situation?" Or better yet, "How do I make sure this doesn't happen again?"

There are nights I still wake up with the sound of the belt and the screams that always followed it echoing in my mind. But the visual that I can never let go of occurred the next morning. Maybe it was the morning after the brussels sprouts night, maybe another morning. It doesn't really matter. There were a lot of "next mornings."

I woke up a little later than Jay, and when I walked into the bathroom, he was in the bathtub. My mom had drawn warm water and filled the tub with Epsom salts. She sat next to the tub close enough to twirl her hand in the water almost like a man-made jacuzzi. She spoke softly to Jay or not at all. When I asked what she was doing, she said that the salts would help the swelling go down. She was trying to hide the welts on Jay's lower back and behind.

I never thought of my dad as a monster. I still don't. I didn't think what he did was out of the ordinary at the time. I grew up in a farm community in Upstate New York. It was the kind of place where you went out in the orchards and cornfields to play and went home again when you heard the bell. Many of my friends and I would share stories about why we got in trouble, but we never spoke about what happened in terms of punishment. Someone might be sporting a bruise or would say their butt was sore. Or someone might say, "I forgot to do my chores. My dad is going to kill me." We all knew what that meant. You did something wrong? Your dad would take care of it. The consequences were understood.

Later in life I learned that when my dad was twelve, his father left. My dad was tasked by his mother to find a job and support the family. He would sneak out to play sports, having to borrow other kids' equipment. Recently, while reflecting on his childhood to me, he cried and said he wished someone had come to his games or that he'd felt that anyone cared. When he was thirty-one, my dad found his father in a homeless shelter. He'd recently gotten married, and I wasn't born yet. He took my grandfather home to their humble two-bedroom apartment until he passed. It's easy to judge parents. It's easy to be a critic. But I think every parent does the best they can with what they know.

Dear Cole, Will, and Jake,

Relationships are the most treasured experiences you will have in life. Each relationship, whether with a partner, friend, family member, or other, should be treated with care and respect. Especially your children, as they will look up to you and learn from your behavior.

Please never let a relationship be managed by fear. I was scared of my dad through most of my childhood. For years, I was afraid to laugh or to get out of my comfort zone. I finally opened up and experienced a lot, but it wasn't easy.

I tried to break the chain in the way I am raising you. I believe I improved the baseline a lot, but you can do even better. If you have children, work to communicate. Set clear boundaries and define consequences.

Pause. Don't react. Ask questions. Listen more. If they are upset or act out verbally or physically, ask why they feel this way. Ask multiple times if you have to, to get to the root feelings...it's always deeper than you initially thought.

It's easier said than done, but it's about progress not perfection. You are the next generation. Do a little better than me and pass it on.

Love, Dad

MAKE YOUR OWN DECISIONS

I wake to the sound of pounding. It sounds like the cracking of wood, like a baseball bat smashing into a large post and splintering. I try to figure out what is going on. The room is dark, but there is a bright light coming from the street through the shade, disorienting me. I sit up in bed and look over to my cousin Mary's bed.

"What was that?" I whisper.

Mary looks back at me, and it's clear she is as scared and confused as I am. I hold my blanket I brought from home as tight as I can to my chest.

It is summer and we're visiting my uncle and his family in the suburbs of Minneapolis. It must be midnight and we have all gone to bed, with the exception of my dad and my uncle, who are downstairs talking. Mary and I open the bedroom door so we can look down the stairway. The light is on and my father and uncle are at the base of the stairs, standing at the closed front door. I can't quite tell if they're arguing, but they're face-to-face and they're both clearly agitated. Later, looking back on it, I will realize they are two brothers asking each other, "What the fuck do we do now?" Because the pounding is coming from the other side of the door, I can see the door shaking. Then suddenly, it pushes off of one of the hinges. My uncle grabs the knob and opens the door.

Tim, my cousin, is framed in the doorway. He is a young teenager, maybe sixteen. It is raining, and he's soaking wet, standing there dressed like a typical seventies teenager with long hair, a jean jacket, and bell bottoms. But there is a look to him that doesn't seem normal. It doesn't seem right. Even as a nine-year-old kid, I can tell something is off. Tim seems angry and frustrated. His fists are clenched, and the look he is giving my father and uncle is one of pure hostility—as if to say this is HIS house—who dares to lock the door and keep him out? I watch my uncle and my dad struggle with him verbally. When they realize Mary and I are watching, they tell us to go back to our room and let this be. I stay up for a while, listening to their voices arguing, screaming, talking.

Eventually, sleep must have won out, because then I woke

up and it was morning. In the sunshine, the entire night had sort of a nightmarish quality to it. Had it really happened? When I came downstairs for breakfast, I could see one of the hinges was off the front door.

I was struck by the fact that all of this had followed what had been a nice evening with my brother and cousins. We had listened to music and argued good-naturedly over which songs were the best, who sang what, etc. I remember when "Sweet Home Alabama" came on the radio, my brother and Tim softly sang along, sitting companionably. I thought Tim was the coolest cat I knew. He was my older cousin and I looked up to him. The memories and feelings from the beginning of that night compared to the end could not have been more different.

Still, the morning was calm. My dad and uncle were already in the backyard, digging a drainage ditch for the house, and I found my mom, who was having coffee with my aunt in the kitchen.

"What happened?" I asked. "Is Tim OK?"

My parents had tried to prep us a little on our way to the visit, telling us that Tim had been having problems with drugs. Still, I had not been prepared for what I had seen, and I couldn't un-see it. What I learned was that Tim had a real problem. He had a drug addiction that was well beyond control. My mother later explained to me that Tim was on "something" that evening, and that wasn't the first time.

This trip was supposed to be a family vacation. Until recently, my aunt, uncle, and cousins had lived near us. We were in and out of each other's houses and spent holidays together. Now, they were in Minnesota and we were still in Upstate New York. I'd been looking forward to the vacation, but now it had taken a dark turn.

We ended up staying an extra few days because my aunt and uncle decided it was time for Tim to get help. I don't know if him banging down the door was the final straw, or if they had always been planning to do it while we were there so my parents could help. I do know that all the younger cousins, including me and my brother, left the house for the day. When we got back, Tim was gone.

Shortly thereafter, two men showed up and began searching the house. They removed light switch covers, unscrewed lightbulbs, and pulled bags of what looked like spices out of the holes. They seemed to know where to look, and everywhere they looked, there was something—a bag that looked like oregano but wasn't. I asked my mom again what was going on, and she was pretty transparent, explaining that Tim had hidden drugs in the house so he could access them when he wanted.

Before we left for home, my mom decided we'd visit Tim in his new "home," and it was an experience that changed me forever. Tim was not in a rehab facility the way you may envision it today when you read about celebrities checking into retreats in Malibu. First of all, I'm not even sure places like that existed in the seventies, but even if they had, this was not Malibu. No. Tim was at a halfway house. It was a shitty house, in a shitty neighborhood, filled with addicts and counselors trying to figure things out. They looked sickly, unclean, and sullen, and as I looked around, I was petrified. Maybe that was my mom's plan, I don't know. But the memory haunted me for a long time.

My mom and I talked a lot about Tim and the drugs, including what drugs do to kids and why people want to take them. She was open about it and explained how addictions occur, how a person starts with something that seems so simple, but then the urge to try something more and experiment with differentiated experiences increases over time. I guess I was lucky in a way that I was scared to death so young. I was convinced that drugs turned you into some kind of monster, which was something I didn't want to see or become.

There were personal consequences I never could have imagined from that experience. Consequences I created for myself. It was a very black-and-white issue for me with no room for nuance. Drugs were bad and I didn't want to be around them. I didn't smoke pot. I didn't take cocaine. I didn't have any desire to try uppers, downers, or any other kind of pill or powder. I was clear on my decision. But here's the catch. I was a teenager in the eighties and drugs were a part of the social landscape. For me, those two realities did not mesh well.

It began in ninth grade. There was a small-town fair going on—one of those traveling fairs with games and rides. Juniors and seniors were throwing a party down the road—in a cornfield, of course, because we grew up in the middle of nowhere. Freshmen and sophomores wanted to be cool and hang out with the older kids, but none of us could drive. Many of us started walking down the road in smaller groups. I was in a group of seven or eight of us. Then a junior, Brian, drove by in his pickup.

"You guys going to the party? Get in the back. We'll bring you."

We all started climbing into the back of his pickup, some of my lifelong best friends included. There was another with us, Mark, who looked at me, paused, and then started crawling back out of the pickup. I could sense it just didn't feel right to him, and I was right there with him. We got a ton of shit from everyone in the back of the truck, but we got out and started walking back to the fair.

For a while, we didn't say a word to each other. Then Mark said, "I just didn't feel comfortable."

"No, neither did I," I said.

"I thought you would go," said Mark.

"Yeah, I thought *you* would go," I answered.

We drifted into sports talk and that was the end of it until we reached the fair, and he said, "I thought you would follow your friends."

"Why would I do that?" I asked, and he smiled.

We never talked about it again. Mark and I were friendly but had never been great friends. This didn't materially change our relationship except there was a level of comfort and respect I had with him, which was unique.

A couple of hours later, the other kids came back to the fair because their parents were picking them up. The seniors were talking to them now as the "cool kids." Mark and I weren't included.

From then on, my best friends from elementary school were throwing, going to, and enjoying parties, many of which involved drugs that I had associated with bad outcomes years before. Since I declined what seemed to be commonplace, having me around was less comfortable for them. I created distance between us, and over time, they just stopped inviting me. I wasn't part of the cool kids anymore. I didn't know what I was.

My neighbor, Steve Trees, who had been my best friend growing up, hosted many of the parties, as his house was the best place to be. All the cool kids in high school would be walking in and my mom and dad would ask me why I wasn't going. I'd say I didn't feel like it, or I didn't feel well that night. Of course, you can only say that once or twice, not twenty times. They knew there was something different. At least my mom did. I never tried to discuss this with my parents as it wasn't an easy subject, nor one I knew how to start. I wish I had, though. I never thought that it was my place to tell on my friends or what they were doing. I was lonely, but I wasn't going to throw them under the bus. To be fair, I don't believe Steve was excluding me because he suddenly didn't like me anymore. Other kids called me scared or said I was too straight, but he knew what people were doing at the party, and he knew it made me uncomfortable. My guess is he just thought it would be easier to keep me away from it. He didn't include me—that was his choice—but he never treated me poorly.

It did make me feel really lonely. I had to create a whole new network of friendships, which were never going to be as deep as the ones with the kids I'd grown up with in elementary school. I became more withdrawn and quiet. I was an observer. Even though my mind was always racing, I didn't say much. My new friends and I would drink beer and have parties in a field, but when my old friends showed up, it just felt awkward and uncomfortable.

It's amazing the implications of a simple decision. In this case, "No, I don't want to do drugs," changed who I hung out with and then changed my behavior. I remember a time in the midst of this when Steve asked me to come to his family's lake house and help with their dock. I don't know if it was his idea or if maybe his dad suggested it, because he noticed we weren't hanging out together anymore.

A group of us went out to the lake house. It was Mr. Trees, Steve, and all my old friends. At this point they had formalized their social circle. It was almost like a fraternity with a name and a handshake and everything. You definitely "belonged" or you didn't. I felt like a distant stranger, as if I'd just been introduced to a group that I had never met before. I wanted to feel like I belonged.

While we were there, Mr. Trees asked for one of us to get in the water and help center the dock. No one would do it because it was so cold. It was March in Upstate New York. The water had to be in the low forties, if not upper thirties at the time. Someone looked at me and said, "Hey,

Lee, you get in and we'll let you be a member of our group." Awkward. I didn't even understand what that meant, but I really didn't care about going into the lake. Mr. Trees seemed to need the help and nobody was making an effort, so what the hell. Maybe I could kill two birds with one stone, right? I thought this was a chance to rebuild what we had lost for so long. I jumped in. It was freezing. I stood there in the lake and helped Mr. Trees center the dock, shaking from the cold. When we were all done, I got out and everyone was giving me pats on the back. Someone handed me a towel and said, "All is good."

I think that was on a Saturday or Sunday. Monday rolled around, and I walked into school smiling, minding my own business. Then one of the boys from the weekend stuck his head in front of my face while I was at my locker.

"Yeah, sorry, we can't let you into the group. Not all of us were there. We didn't all agree. Because of that, it wasn't fair to the group. So, you're not really in it. We're sorry about that, but you have to have everyone there." A few of the other boys were there, too. Some of them smiled and others laughed a little bit as they walked away. That experience wasn't easy to understand or accept, but it was a gift of awareness that assisted me in helping others to this day.

It was not a bullying situation, but I became quieter, more withdrawn. I stuck to myself.

One afternoon, my brother came home from the library and said, "You know, I was talking to a few girls at school. They said Lee was one of the kindest and cutest boys in the entire school, but he doesn't speak often. If he would, he could have anything."

I laughed at it and thought it was such a compliment they thought I was cute because I didn't see myself that way. Deep down, it also really hurt. *If they only knew I enjoy asking questions and listening to people,* I thought. I was quiet because I liked to hear what other people had to say, and I didn't believe people wanted to hear my opinion. *If they only knew.* So, it made me withdraw even more. I figured I would just keep quiet and stay out of everyone's way. The less I was seen, the better. That's how I carried out my last few years of high school, executing the best I could athletically and getting a lot of recognition and recruitment interest from colleges but remaining quiet. I felt no one wanted me around, but it was my own mind that created this prison.

It's amazing how one experience so many years ago, a single simple decision, can have a ripple effect so many decades later. I was scared to death to see what my cousin went through. He went through many more halfway houses. He continued to struggle with addiction, drifting in and out of small jobs. He eventually got his act together, and from what I heard he is doing OK, but it took a tremendous toll on his family. When people try to use drugs to change their life, to make it feel better, to alter reality, there's consequences. The consequences aren't just for the individual who chose that path, but for everyone around them and not just immediate family members. It extends so much farther beyond that.

My uncle died a few years ago. He was really loved. He made me laugh, and my dad, too. I think my dad misses him very much. I sometimes wonder how much pain Tim created for his father with the decisions he made at such a young age. At the same time, I wonder about the other side of the story. Would Tim say my uncle had been physically, emotionally, and intellectually present for him? That's something I'll never know. Tim's decisions hurt himself and his family, and, while no one could have predicted this, least of all me, those decisions radically changed my thoughts and set me on a path.

The fact is, not all decisions are easy. Even easy decisions, or decisions we are completely confident are right, can have consequences and repercussions. Sometimes, I wonder if I hadn't seen that halfway house, would my life have been different? Would my decisions have been different? Would they have been better? Worse? The same? I don't know.

I don't blame anyone or anything for what I experienced

during those years. The decisions are all mine. In some ways, I wonder if my complete rejection of drugs was closed-minded, or it if influenced me to be closed-minded. If I couldn't try a little pot because I was convinced I would end up at a halfway house, what else was I saying no to? The point isn't whether my decision was right or wrong. It's about awareness that no decision happens in a vacuum. Tim's decisions showed me a side of drugs that haunted me for years. My decisions caused me to withdraw into myself during my high school years. I made another decision when I was going to college. I chose to just let go and be myself. That decision changed me again.

Dear Cole, Will, and Jake,

I don't want to sound like a parent telling my sons not to do drugs. I think everyone will say that to you and that's not the takeaway from this chapter.

I'm not here to tell you what's right and wrong. I'm not here to tell you what you should and shouldn't do. I'm asking you to be aware of who you are and don't give anyone else the power to define you or your life.

I was once asked, whom should I listen to out of the one hundred people lined up to speak with me—the ninety-nine who said bad things about me, or the one who said great things about me? The answer is none of them. Listen to yourself. You know you are worth it.

Be you.

Love, Dad

LESSON #3

———

TRUST YOUR GUT

There was something different about Diane. In seventh grade, we held hands and then the following morning she sent me a note informing me, "We're not dating any-more." Such is seventh-grade love. That was it for a few years. Then, during my senior year of high school, I looked through an open window in the school searching for my buddies (who were late), and I saw her walking down the hallway. There was still something different about her.

Diane grew up with a single mom in a small apartment on the upper level of a duplex in town. The apartment had two bedrooms, one of which Diane shared with her sister, Caroline. We were out in the middle of nowhere, a farm community. She was in the "village" part of it, which had one flashing red light and a bar called "Bar." Diane's father had a severe drinking problem, and her mother moved them away when Diane was young. It gave them a better chance to eliminate the violence, screaming, and difficulties that accompanied him. Mrs. Wood, Diane's mom, met a wonderful man that felt like a father to Diane. He tried to fill the shoes of the father who had never made an attempt to be in Diane's, or her sister's, life. Mrs. Woods worked as a receptionist at Kent. She worked very hard, drove an old car that barely started in the morning, and just got her, hopefully, to work and back. But she was always happy. I never saw her cry or be overly stern with her girls.

Caroline was a studious, thoughtful, caring, obedient, and wonderful daughter. Diane, on the other hand, was a rebellious teenager. While she had gotten into a lot of things that probably most moms and dads wouldn't want, Diane always knew when to say enough was enough. I always thought she was really cute, but it was more than that. There was just something about her, and I believed she could accomplish so much if she would just give herself the opportunity. I couldn't explain it. It was just instinct.

I started dating Diane at the end of my senior year. My parents thought it was a foolish time to start a relationship, since I would be leaving in the fall for college. I believe my dad viewed Diane as someone who came from nothing and who would be more of a burden on me than someone who supported me and my goals. My mom was always kind to her, but I don't think she took the relationship very seriously given that college would be starting soon. And me? I just knew that Diane was someone worth having in my life. I trusted her. She believed in me when no one else did.

We did break things off when I was in college, but it was amicable, and we stayed friends. In fact, I suffered a bad injury in college (more on this in the next chapter), and she was always there for me, visiting, doing her best to help me get through it. I went my way in college, and she went hers and became a hair stylist. I don't think she particularly wanted to do that, but she had been cutting hair in high school and felt like it was a way she could earn a living for a time. She lived in Nantucket in the summers and came back home to Upstate New York in the winters, eventually moving to Florida during the cold months.

When I was finishing college, we ran into each other again. For the next few years, we dated on and off. The core of our relationship was a deep friendship, and so dating came and went, but we were consistently in each other's lives. As we rekindled our relationship near the close of my senior year, I could tell Diane was going a little stir crazy. It wasn't about where she was living, it was about the way life was going. I wanted to see her thriving. I questioned what she enjoyed doing. Did she love her work? Love her life? And slowly, subtly, thoughtfully, I would just remind her—I thought she could do anything if she gave it a chance. Why not try college? She would refuse and make fun of herself and say, "No, that's not for me." I'd leave her alone but come back to it time and again.

"Give yourself a chance," I said. "I think you're pretty sharp. I don't think you realize how much potential you have. Give it a try." I never told her to go to college, but I always prompted her and gave her my opinion that she was good enough, if not better, than most of the kids I knew at university. I was gauging this on wit, sarcasm, thoughtfulness, how she handled money, and more.

Time continued to pass. I completed my undergraduate degree and went on to become a graduate assistant at the University of Albany. I was coaching while completing my master's degree, making no money, living paycheck to paycheck. Any extra bills were on a credit card that, quite frankly, didn't have much of a line of credit.

One day, Diane called me to say, "I've enrolled in junior college, near Mom's apartment." For the next two years, she earned straight A's and her perspective began to shift. I kept telling her, "I'm not surprised. You can do this."

A professor who served as her mentor told her the same things she had heard from me—she could do so much more if she gave herself a chance. At some point, Diane began to believe. I like to think that my words helped her recognize the truth of the professor's thoughts. Something began to shift and she realized she did have an aptitude for learning. There were opportunities out there she had never considered before. By the end of her second year, she started to think, "I can do this. I could have a life that's different than the way my mom lived and the way I grew up."

I suggested she apply to different universities to continue her education. She applied to Colgate, University of South Carolina, Bucknell, and the list goes on and on. With her grades, her work ethic, and her mentor's recommendation, she was accepted to every one of them. Ultimately, she picked South Carolina because she wanted to pursue international business, and they also gave her an academic scholarship.

When it came time for her to enroll in her first classes, I traveled with her down to the university. You can imagine going from a small junior college to a school with thirty thousand students and having no idea where to go or what to do. She broke down and cried right in the middle of the quad. Everyone was in the gymnasium with paper ballots, registering for classes. It looked like a circus that had gone all wrong.

"This isn't for me. I can't do this," Diane said.

I responded, "Hold on, let's walk to the admissions building."

We entered the building and found this thoughtful staff member who sat Diane down and gave her a few tissues and a glass of water, realizing how upset she was. I explained the situation, and this woman patiently went through the whole process with Diane. It was a simple reminder that no matter how big the world seems to be, if you are thoughtful and ask politely, there is always someone to help.

My instinct on Diane was right, as she began a very successful run at the University of South Carolina.

During the times Diane and I were dating, my father, whenever he saw me, would have something negative to say. "What are you doing with that girl?" he'd ask. "She means nothing. She is from a broken family. She's never going to amount to anything. She's a hairdresser. She started college late."

My father was trying to protect me from becoming responsible for someone who wouldn't be able to help financially, from his perspective, but there's so much more to a relationship than that.

I remember one night at the dinner table when he actually said, "Who is this girl? She must be really good in bed."

I threw my chair back, grabbed my father (it was the only

time in my life I did so), picked him up off his chair, and pushed him into the wall, making an indentation. As soon as I realized what I was doing, I let go of him, knowing how wrong it was. I wasn't going to be him. He cursed me out, said a lot of things that weren't positive, and I just walked away.

My father never said a positive thing about Diane. "Get rid of this joker," was his common refrain. He didn't always have positive things to say about me either. If Diane was around and heard him say something negative about me, she would stick up for me, point right in his face and yell back to him. She was always defending me when I did not defend myself. Many years later, maybe fifteen years later, my father told me, unsolicited, "You know what? I was wrong about Diane. I was very wrong. And you were right. Perhaps I should have listened to you." It's the only time in my life I can recall my father apologizing and admitting he was wrong.

To be honest, he wasn't the only one who was negative. In graduate school, my friends and colleagues would look at me sort of quizzically when it came to my relationship with Diane. They would say things like, "Isn't she still in junior college? You are building a career. You need to break that off." Or my mom, who was always kind to Diane but still worried, would say, "Where do you think this is actually going?"

The people around me didn't see what I did. It would have been easy for me to turn to Diane and say, "Well, good luck," and leave it at that, but I knew she could be more, and I wanted to be around to see it. I shielded her from the negative comments I received. The only message she ever heard from me was, "I think you have bigger things ahead of you."

When Diane finally started at South Carolina, she was not just going to college but working two jobs to pay for her apartment and the other costs of living. At the end of her senior year, I got to witness the success I had envisioned many years ago as she was recruited by some of the top investment banks. She accepted a job on the mortgage desk of a sell side firm. Over the ensuing years, she became one of their top traders and took on many more roles at the bank. She would often call me and say how surprised she was, how excited she was, how thrilled she was, but she never promoted herself. There was this deep insecurity that she just wasn't good enough. Every time I only had one thing to say: "You are as good, if not better, than anyone else I run into. You can do anything. Just give it the best chance." Eventually, she also earned an MBA, and her life continued to reflect success earned through her patience, work ethic, sincerity, and genuine thought.

Dear Cole, Will, and Jake,

If you believe in someone, don't let anyone tell you differently. Instinct is one of the most powerful tools you have. Believe in your gut. Believe in what you feel. Listen to the ones your gut tells you to. It might change your life.

I often think of Diane and wish her the very best. She's married with two boys, and I'm so happy for her. I think we both needed each other at the time, just to tell each other we weren't lost, we weren't worthless. You'll find that person in your life. Don't push them away. There are some amazing people out there. At the very worst, even if they don't live up to all the dreams or ideals you had for them, I'm willing to bet they'll end up in a much better place just because you believed in them.

I love you,

Dad

FIND YOUR INNER STRENGTH

As I lie on my back looking up, I see patches of clear blue sky between the grill of my football helmet. The university band is silent. A moment ago, I was sprinting towards a sweep option tailback coming out of the backfield. Now, images are coming in and out of my line of sight. Some I recognize, some I don't. People are asking me questions, but what I hear is basically the voice of Charlie Brown's teacher. Wah. Wah. Wah. I'm trying to figure out what's going on. I can feel others around me, coaches and referees off to my left. I try to turn my head to look around, but I can't. I try to stand up, but I can't. I am starting to realize that nothing works. My brain is saying, "Get up, try to move," but my body is not responding.

"What's going on?" I manage to ask.

"You were unconscious. Do you feel anything?" someone asks me. I don't think I answer.

I watch people enter and exit the periphery of my vision, but I can't move anything except my eyes. Someone tells me they have called for support to bring me off the field and evaluate me. That can't be good. I am starting to compute what is happening, and all I want to know is, "How bad is this?" But I can't speak, can't ask, so no one answers that question for me. It's hard to even recognize anyone. The coaches, trainers, referees, they're all blurred together. It's not like I am surrounded by immediate family. It is profound isolation.

They lift me, and the scenes in my periphery change. That's the only reason I know we are moving, because I can't feel it. I see the ambulance as they load me in. I've completely shut down verbally, and I'm focused on evaluating my situation. What is the problem? How can I solve it? I'm taking in as much information as I can. I will learn later that this trait is at the core of my personality. I observe, almost absorb, what is around me before I react.

Even with the sirens on, it will take us thirty minutes to reach the nearest major hospital. I lie there, wondering what is going to happen. I'm still wearing my football helmet. I don't really feel it, but I can see the face mask is still there.

Once I'm at the hospital, they remove the helmet by unscrewing the mask and explain that they are cutting off all of my equipment. Slowly, they are feeding me information. They ask me if I have any feeling as they remove each piece of equipment. I don't. At some point, my mom and dad enter the room. I'm still quiet. I could speak, but I have nothing to say. I am absorbing what is happening around me, what is happening to me. I have no reference point for a situation like this. *What the fuck is going on?* I wonder.

I spend the next seven to nine hours cycling through CAT scans, MRIs, and X-rays. In the moment, I don't know how much time is passing. It is only later when they tell me how long it was. Finally, someone is ready to talk to me. A doctor leans over my face so I can see him.

"Lee, I can describe your injuries very formally, but the reality is, you broke your neck," he says. I hear a loud crash, but the doctor does not move and does not break eye contact with me.

"What was that?" I ask.

"Your mother just fainted," he explains. "Your dad is helping her up."

I smile a little at that and then focus again on the doctor as he goes on with his assessment.

"A number of vertebrae are compressed, and your muscles have frozen to basically create a cast. We don't know what's going to happen. I see three possible outcomes. One, the muscles come off the bone structure safely and you fully recover. Two, the reaction of the bones and muscles release in such a way that you have a partial recovery, from the waist up. Or three, the worst-case scenario, the muscles sever the nerves when they release, and you end up fully paralyzed."

I can feel tears rolling down my face, but I need to focus. The doctor continues, "I'm telling you all this because you need to understand where we are. We don't yet know what the outcome will be."

I heard everything he said, and I am starting to understand just how bad this is. Really. Fucking. Bad. But at the same time, I know instantly that there is only one possible outcome—full recovery.

From that moment on, I never even considered that the paralysis would be permanent or that the recovery could be only partial. Sure, I had my moments of fear and doubt, but those moments were never as strong as my conviction that I would get better.

Over the course of the next six months, I completed an intense recovery that was life-changing in every way—

physically, mentally, and emotionally. It began with the smallest of movements. For two and a half days, I lay in the hospital waiting to see what my muscles would do. I was motionless and there were no signs of recovery. At that point, no one knew what the outcome was going to be. At first, my mind was distracted by trivial questions: Were my friends missing me? What was my girlfriend doing right now? Did we win the game? Who would come visit me?

But as the hours ticked by and I still couldn't move, my mind shifted from the superficial to deeper questions. *If I'm not the sure-footed, confident athlete I was two days ago, who am I now?*

Nurses came in and out of the room and left fresh water, which they would periodically bring to me with a straw so I could drink it. Two and a half days into the waiting, I wanted some water, but the nurse wasn't around. Without giving it any thought, I tried to move my hand to pick it up, and my hand actually moved. It moved! I began screaming as loudly as I could (remember, I couldn't press any of the call buttons). The nurse came running into my room, but I didn't stop yelling. I shifted my eyes down to my hand and moved it again. She yelled for a doctor and she then began encouraging me.

"Keep doing it! See how much you can do!"

Over the next twelve to thirteen hours, I experienced a slow nerve response across my entire body. Basically, everything was slowly coming back. Cue more CAT scans, MRIs, and X-rays, followed by the doctor coming to me with an update.

"We have really good, but cautious news. The muscles are relaxing from the bone structure. So far, so good. Let's hope the positive nature of the process continues—that the bones don't sever any nerves as they come off."

I was numb, but now that feeling was coming back, I could also feel the pain. I had very deep pain in my neck. I still couldn't move my right arm, and my right leg had very slow response activity. The doctor pointed out that I still had multiple broken bones that needed to fuse. The hope was that if they were splintered "well," they would re-heal, but concerns remained about my future.

Now that the doctors knew recovery was a possibility, the hard work was about to begin. It was decision time. There were two approaches for the next stage of recovery, and they were both difficult. The first option was a full body cast, which entailed me living in and out of the hospital for the next six months. The second option was a halo brace, which is a metal brace that circles your head and is attached to the skull. Four pins are screwed into your skull, two above your eyebrows to keep it in place, and two in the back. Metal rods connect from the screws to the brace around your shoulders creating a "halo." The intent is to keep the bones in your neck from moving.

When I saw the picture of the halo, I basically said there was no fucking way I was wearing it and I wanted the cast. The doctor knew it was a big decision and wanted me to be thoughtful about all of the pros and cons. In his view, the benefit of the halo brace was that I would be able to live in the comfort of my home, surrounded by my family and my own space, which could be helpful for my mental state. He invited another patient with a halo brace in to speak with me. The visit only reinforced my decision. All he had to do was walk through the door. It was not for me. That poor son of a bitch.

So now, I was looking at six months of living mainly in the hospital and working harder than I had ever worked before in order to get my mobility back. I was surrounded by quadriplegics who were never going to walk again, no matter how hard they tried. That was not my future, not in my mind. Very quickly, I realized that the opportunity before me was a gift. I was convinced I would recover. When I looked around, I realized, "Wow, I thought I had it tough, but look at these people. I am really lucky." There was a five-year-old child on my floor who was never going to walk again, and there was an eight-year-old boy down the hall who had been in a car that got hit by a drunk driver. He was going to be a quadriplegic for the rest of his life, and his mother had died in the accident. Yes, I was lucky.

Within the first week, I was constantly reminded how fortunate I was. Many of these folks were there because of unlucky circumstances—accidents on the job, drunk drivers, etc. What were they going home to? I was young and strong, and I had an opportunity. From day one, my only question was, "When can I start walking?" The doctors, nurses, and therapists all explained there was a build-up to that point, and it was an intense process. I was ready. Start. Let's go.

That is not to say, of course, that there were not dark days and darker nights (the nights were always harder than the days). There were. You never know how important family is until a crisis hits, but family can't fix everything and doesn't play every role. I was surprised by how few friends came to visit me. I wasn't quite sure how to take that. I had thought I had good friends. My self-worth took a hit. Was there something wrong with me that they didn't care I was in the hospital? A few came to visit and through them I heard that others had come while I was sleeping or "couldn't bear to see me in that state." It bothered me. Several people I expected to show up never did, but there were happy surprises, too, where people I didn't expect came to visit. It caused me to think long and hard about my views on friendship. What did I value in a friend? What did I value in life?

One group of friends raised money on campus to send me flowers and chocolates. They actually raised a good amount of cash, but when they totaled it all, they decided instead to throw a keg party, justifying it with comments like, "Well, that's what Lee would really want us to do." Of course, they didn't ask me. Months later, some people found out and were angry, but the vast majority of the people at the party knew where all that beer money had come from. Were those the kind of people I called friends? I can look back now and say they were college kids who made a mistake, but at the time, it was hard to swallow.

Another eye-opener was my girlfriend's reaction. She was the "it" girl on campus, the one every eighties movie, like *Can't Buy Me Love*, is about. She was beautiful and the captain of the cheerleading squad. We had been dating for months, and in college, "months" is a lifetime. I kept waiting for her to visit, but she never came. Finally, another friend told me that she couldn't deal with my injuries and had, in fact, already moved on to start dating another football player, a teammate. Wow. I was shocked. And hurt. Again, it made me think. What was I really looking for in a relationship?

The days flowed from one to the next. There were different trainings, different therapies, different people. Over time, I realized that the only constant was me. All of these people were offering me tremendous support, but I was the difference maker. I was the one who had to find the strength to get up every day and fight for my recovery. I was the one who had to have the unwavering commitment to getting better. No one could do it for me. Literally. It was a simultaneously liberating and terrifying lesson.

I got stronger every day. While encouraging, the professionals were also cautious. They explained there were certain activities that would never be available to me again. Yes, I had skied competitively when I was younger, but I should not expect to ever ski again. Their words did nothing but deepen my commitment. "I get it, but that's not me," I would think. "Fuck that."

Since that experience, I have made a practice of going to extremes if I feel like it is the right thing to do, and if you are in my vicinity, I'll pull you along with me. Professionally, it has led to some great wins. It has also led to some big headaches and people shaking their heads at me and saying, "He just doesn't get it." That's OK, too. Like I said, I don't have it all figured out. I only know what I've learned about myself.

One clear lesson from my rehabilitation experience was to rely on myself. I think there are positives and negatives to that life approach. I'm not analyzing it, just stating that's where I ended up. I also think I grew up faster and more thoughtfully than I would have if this had not happened to me. Prior to the injury, I thought I had it all figured out. I was arrogant. I was achieving national recognition as an athlete, I earned good grades, I was dating the cheerleader. I had it all. Right? My injury made me realize that old joke is true—if you want a good laugh, tell God what you're doing tomorrow.

After the injury and rehab, I realized that not only did I not have it all figured out, my compass on what really mattered in life had not been pointing true north. It made me wonder what I still didn't know yet. To this day, I wake up wondering how much I still don't know.

Dear Cole, Will, and Jake,

There will be moments in your life when you are the only one who can do it. My hope for you is that you fail often and early in life to build resilience and that you have a strong support network of family, partners, and friends. But it doesn't change the facts. No matter who is around and supporting you, the only way to manifest whatever outcome you are trying to achieve is through your own determination and energy. It has to come from inside you.

It's a hard lesson and sometimes people live their whole lives without understanding it. I feel lucky that I learned it so early.

I love you,

Dad

LESSON #5

___

UNDERSTAND HOW OTHERS SEE YOU, BUT DON'T LET THEM DEFINE YOU

Fast forward. Rewind. Pause. Write. Fast forward again. Too far. Rewind. Pause. Write.

I'm watching football tape, alone, on a Saturday night, in the film room of the university where I'm coaching. We have state-of-the-art technology, which at the time is VHS tapes, two big, blocky TV inserts, and a control panel with buttons larger than my fingers. A graduate assistant drove to the airport to pick up the tapes earlier today, and my job is to break them down.

Breaking down tapes means watching a game film the

other team exchanged and, bit by bit, play by play, analyzing tendencies. What did they do on first down and short? What about on third down and long? What was their formation package? When do they run a quarterback draw? When do they use the shotgun formation? As I virtually splice each play on film, I record my perspective in written notes. I'm trying to assess the competition's tendencies, so we can build a defensive game plan. As a defensive coach, I am focused on watching their offense, asking myself, "How would I defend against their style of play?" Eventually, I will present my summary to the rest of the coaches and we will devise a scheme to offset theirs.

As I sit in the dark, the head coach walks by. He's been at the program for many years, and right now, he is the only other one around. Everyone else is still out celebrating our win earlier that day. I had a couple of beers with them after the game but then came back to the film room. Someone always has to break down the films, and I had volunteered. At twenty-two, I don't have a wife or kids, and I'm happy to spend my time looking at the plays.

"What are you doing?" Coach asks.

"I'm breaking down their offense," I say.

"Is that the best plan?" he asks.

"Excuse me?" I answer, not sure where this is going.

"I have a different thought," he says. "If you really want to be prepared and give a useful summary to the other coaches, perhaps reverse your thinking. You need to watch the film we sent them of us and break down how they would defend against every type of play. If you were them, how would you attack us? Break *that* down, play by play, then you can break down their film. That's how we create a thoughtful, effective game strategy."

"That's twice the work," I observe.

"Yup. That's life," he answers as he walks away.

That lesson has stuck with me for life. Though it came from an industry unrelated to the one I'm in now, it has been applicable for my entire life. It was probably my single greatest lesson from my days as a coach, but it was not my only one.

I loved coaching. I ate, slept, and drank coaching. I could be up at five o'clock in the morning and not get to bed until midnight that night, and I would be excited to get up at five o'clock in the morning the next day and get back to it again.

After I broke my neck, I couldn't play football anymore.

I lost my scholarship and ended up transferring schools. Though I couldn't play anymore, I had grown so much as a person while rehabbing from my injury, and I felt I had a lot to offer. There was a prep school not far from my new university that had a coach I had played for. I volunteered at that school and received my first taste of coaching. I loved helping individuals meet their personal best. I felt I had something unique to give following my injury. I could tell these kids how precious each moment was and how quickly it could all go. Every minute matters. To this day, I sometimes get letters from athletes I coached telling me about how my perspective influenced their lives.

Coaching had nothing to do with my undergrad degree, but I knew I wanted to do it professionally. I had no connections, so I started writing letters to every Division I school I could think of. There was no email at this time. It was me, putting stamps on letters and hoping for the best. I told these coaches my story and explained why I wanted to coach. Surprisingly, I was accepted by many schools.

My first professional coaching gig was at the Coach's Cradle in Upstate New York. I was a graduate assistant funded by the football program. They paid for my education, and I coached for them. They owned me. I was up at the crack of dawn working for them and I went to bed thinking about work. I lived in one room with another coach/graduate assistant. We worked twenty-four/seven, finding a few hours at night for classes. We worked weekends as barbacks or bouncers to make money. We never went out. We never had weekends off. One hundred percent of our time was accounted for, and most of it was dedicated to coaching football. And I loved it. When you really love what you do, there's no such thing as the Sunday Night Blues. You want to be at work because it doesn't feel like work. And if you're lucky, the people around you feel the same way. We never cared about going out. We would simply have a beer in our office. We were already with all our friends, talking about what we loved the most, so what did it matter where we were?

The fly in the ointment was my dad's perspective. It was always negative. "When are you going to grow up? You're not making any money. You don't have a real job. This is just a dream that will end badly," he would say.

I remember one occasion when I was coaching and we had won big. We had beaten the number three team in the NCAA Division I Football Bowl Subdivision (FBS). Everyone was going out to celebrate, but I had promised my parents I would visit them, and I didn't want to cancel. I got in the car and started the drive home. This time, I was looking forward to hearing what my dad would say. It had been a nationally televised game, and I was confident he had watched it. I was ready to hear, for once, that I had done a good job.

When I arrived, he was watching a different football game. At first, he didn't say anything. I could wait. I was patient and I figured it was probably hard for him to admit he had been wrong. After a few minutes, he left the room.

When he came back, he settled in his chair and said, "So when are you going to stop being such a fucking loser and get a real job?"

I stopped cold, at a loss for words. *Holy shit*, I thought, *this is never going to stop. I can't win.* The constant negativity began to eat at me and, worse, it made me start to doubt myself. Little by little, questions would rise in my mind. Was I a loser? Was this a pipe dream?

During this same time period, my brother had settled into a professional role as a financial analyst. From time to time, he would fly me out for a visit and his boss always tried to recruit me. It was flattering. Then one night I was in bed, running plays in my head and watching the snow blowing outside the window. I had a ski cap on because the room was so cold, and I suddenly saw myself through my dad's eyes. And the doubt kicked in. Was I a loser? I decided maybe he was right, and I should do something else. The next day, I called my brother and asked if he could get me an interview with his firm. I arranged it for the end of the season. Before I knew it, they were offering me $21,000 a year along with subsidizing my living expenses. I thought I had just found easy street. I couldn't wait to tell my dad. But there was a part of me, a gut feeling, that told me this was not a good decision. I ignored it. I called my dad and let his excitement be stronger than my misgivings. He thought it was a brilliant move, and I figured I must be doing the right thing. I pushed the gut feeling down and didn't feel it again for years.

Here's the thing: that gut feeling was right. This was not a good decision for me. Doing what you love might not lead to great financial success, but that's the wrong metric to gauge your life by. I still miss coaching. I can't wait to get back to coaching and teaching, but when I get there is another discussion. The truth is, I doubted myself so much that I left something I loved to make someone else happy.

Dear Cole, Will, and Jake,

In today's society focused so much on everyone else, please watch your own game film. Until you understand how you are viewed by others, whether that is the competition, a client, a potential partner, or whomever, until you can honestly identify your own strengths and challenges, you can't build an effective plan. You will always be reacting.

It's not easy. You need to look in the mirror and be impartial and honest. Then, if you see something you don't like, you can address it. Looking at information just one way, even if that way is the industry standard, it's not enough. You must understand how others see you if you really want to be effective.

Don't let others define who you are. You are the only one who should hold that power.

I love you,

Dad

LESSON #6

CHOOSE YOUR PARTNER CAREFULLY

"I'm not going," my wife says, breaking the silence. "I just... can't. I'm going to spend the time by myself."

"What?" I respond. "You're kidding, right? You're telling me now?"

We're supposed to be leaving for a two-week family vacation to Nantucket. I've just finished packing the car, and Cole (age seven), Will (five), and Jake (two) are buckled in and ready to go.

I realize it's not a joke. My wife isn't coming with us. I can't think of what to say or do, so I simply turn and get in the truck, beginning a six-hour drive that will include some very challenging hours. I don't see any other options of how to handle it, so I just keep going.

For the first hour, I dodge questions from the kids about why Mom isn't in the car, making things up like, "Mom didn't feel well," or, "She said she will join us later." Eventually, the kids stop asking and I can start to try to process what is happening. Kelly, a combination of nanny, house cleaner, and quiet support who has helped us with the boys since Jake's arrival, is also with us, but she heard the announcement the same time as me and isn't going to say a word. So, the car is fairly quiet and I get lost in my thoughts.

I've been through a lot in my life. I broke my neck. I rehabbed from paralysis. I've been diagnosed with cancer (more on that later). But this was the most differentiated six hours of my life because I suddenly realized that everything, my entire life, was connected to this relationship. My marriage was at the core of every life decision—my children, where I lived, where I worked, how I spent my free time—everything. If my marriage wasn't going to work out, what did that mean? As I tried to manage my emotions, questions tumbled over themselves, fighting for space in my brain. If we weren't together, where would the kids be? Would we have to fight about that? Would we sell the house? If we didn't sell the house, who would get it? Why was this happening? What the hell was I going to tell the boys on my own for the next *two* weeks? Above it all, over and over, how did I get here? Every evening during that "boys" vacation, I would fall asleep in one of my sons' beds and wake up in the middle of the night wondering where I was.

The question of "How did I get here?" is the one I want to come back to, because it is the question I spent the most time analyzing, not just on that drive, but for years after. Who you choose as a partner in life, and how you sustain that relationship, is the single most important decision you will ever make. It impacts your day-to-day happiness, your finances, where you live, how you spend your free time, who you spend holidays with, everything. If that partnership unravels, all the rest unravels, too.

My marriage ended well before I knew. Officially, it ended a year after that vacation. I spent untold hours thinking about it—what I had done well, and where I had failed.

When my wife and I were living in Colorado, shortly after Will was born, I received a job offer in New York City. We decided I would take it and we'd move to New Jersey, because she had grown up there and wanted to be close to her parents and live in that community. Princeton is a terrific place, but it's a killer commute to New York. Assuming everything was working as it was supposed to, I spent four hours a day commuting. Any commuter to New York City will tell you that it is a rare day when everything goes according to schedule. That commute took a toll on me, and I also think it took a toll on us. I thought my work was giving something to the family that was valued enough to justify my absence. I'm not sure anymore if that's true.

Did I travel for work too much? Was that how I got here?

Plenty of other questions plagued me as well. Did we get enough help for ourselves as individuals for problems that were outside of the scope of the relationship? Did I follow my own ears-to-mouth ratio advice and listen twice as much as I talked? Did I stop trusting my partner enough to show the real me? Had I been vulnerable enough? Had she stopped trusting me with the real her? And if she had, did I notice? Did I stop asking questions because it was easier to ignore the problems? Did I pay attention to the warning signals that things weren't going well or that we weren't really a good match? Did I listen hard enough when people I cared for shared concerns? Why hadn't I realized that we didn't really share a lot of common interests? Did I stay genuine to myself in this relationship?

Pondering all these questions made me realize no one had ever told me how much this decision mattered, or what kinds of things to consider. I got plenty of advice on how to choose a school, how to choose a career, and what kind of community to raise my kids in. You name it, people had advice. But no one ever talks about how you choose a mate. Yet it matters more than anything else.

Dear Cole, Will and Jake,

When you choose a partner, be thoughtful. Watch your own game film. Watch their game film. I think there are four broad categories to consider when you are evaluating a long-term relationship:

***Physical**—Especially in the beginning of a relationship, physical factors play a large role. People can argue with this, but it's my opinion (and if they want to argue, they can write their own damn book). Particularly for men, I think the first category used to assess a partner will always be physical attraction. I might cringe at that fact, but it doesn't make it less true. I think 75–80 percent of the reason men are with someone in the beginning of the relationship is attraction. Over time, this factor will decrease in importance.*

***Intellectual**—Being intellectually stimulated by someone who challenges you to think will be a benefit to you over time. Do you operate on the same level, yes or no? Because if you don't, communication gets much harder.*

***Emotional**—An emotional connection comes from paying attention, from listening, from asking questions. It takes time and can get stronger over months and years, but you need to make sure it exists. In a relationship, you each need to be aware of who the other is as a person.*

***Spiritual**—if your religious perspectives are vastly different, you need* to address it. Try to move towards each other or at least be willing to share and partake in each other's religious beliefs. Be ready to respect their views, to understand why they think and feel a certain way, and support them on some level beyond simply acknowledging their beliefs.

Beyond those categories, I would offer some other advice about sustaining a relationship that I learned the hard way.

First, live where you work. Second, listen and speak according to the ratio of ears to mouth—that is, listen twice as much as you speak. Third, don't change who you are for someone else.

As I've said before, I don't have everything figured out, but I learned some lessons the hard way, and I am hoping that my experiences will help you be thoughtful in how you evaluate and manage your own relationships. While I hope you don't go through what your mother and I did, you'll be OK if you do.

Finally, I want to add that I'll never regret what I received from this relationship: you boys. My greatest gifts. Ever. (Although there are moments...;))

I love you,

Dad

LESSON #7

REGULARLY REEVALUATE WHO YOU ARE AND WHAT YOU WANT

I sit down in a chair I've sat in many times before and look at my boss. We have sat in this office debating issues, solving problems, making plans, defining strategy. But he is more than a boss; he is also a friend. We have sat in this office just as many times talking about our kids, with me asking him for advice. In fact, six weeks ago, he and his children spent the weekend with me and my family at our summer home on vacation.

This is hard. My palms are sweaty. "I'm resigning," I say. He looks away and doesn't look back. This man trusted me, believed in me, gave me opportunities, and supported me from day one. I feel I've disappointed him profoundly.

For a heartbeat, there is total silence and then he says, "I know I'm going to regret how I handled this when I look back at it one day." He stands up and turns his back to me, calling out, "Please go straight to HR. You can't go back to your office." I want to say so many things, to explain my decision, to apologize, to defend, but I can't. I do what he asks. I get up and leave.

This place was good to me. It is a good firm, where I was respected, well-compensated, and surrounded by smart people with pride and integrity. Leaving is hard. I have nothing but positive things to say in my exit interview. My friend in HR tells me he is sorry to see me go and, somewhere, there is a voice inside me already wondering if I'm sorry to see me go, too. I am escorted out of the building, which is standard practice when you leave for the competition in financial services.

I begin walking and wait for the relief. The hard part is over. Now, I can celebrate this decision. I am going to a competitor that has aggressively recruited me for a year. I have been asked to lead change in a company that is already succeeding. Most important for my day-to-day life, my commute will drop from two hours each way to just fifteen minutes. For the first time ever, if I need to get to one of my sons' schools quickly, I can actually get there. I can run out at lunch for a teacher conference. This is a good decision. Isn't it? But I'm still waiting for the relief.

It's been thirty minutes since I left my former office on Park Avenue, and I realize I have only walked one city block. I find a bench and sit down and list, again, all the reasons why this was such a smart decision. The opportunity. The commute. And, still, I wait for the excitement. Or at least the relief. Instead, I realize I'm trying to convince myself.

I've made this decision for all the wrong reasons. I didn't watch my own game film. I was lured by the money and the flattery. And the commute—I will give myself that one at least, that one is real. But I didn't need a different opportunity right now. I liked my job and the people I worked with—people I considered friends. I made a really nice living already. I didn't need a higher salary.

I come to terms with the fact that instead of relief all I feel is sadness and confusion. I look at my watch and am surprised that I have spent an hour on this bench. I reassure myself that saving four hours a day from commuting and being so much closer to the kids will be worth it. I will make it work.

In financial services when you are moving to a competitor firm, there is a waiting period before you can start your new job. In this case, my waiting period was three months. It was basically an extended vacation. I spent time with my boys and began to mentally prepare for the new job.

Whether I had made the decision for the right reasons or not, I was in it now. How was I going to succeed?

Just before the end of the three months, I met an executive at the new firm for breakfast. We covered the basics of what he was looking to accomplish. It was a thoughtful, fact-based conversation. I was being brought into a part of the business that was in transformation. Change was both needed and expected. But there was an undercurrent there, a sense of urgency that had never been addressed in my many recruiting conversations. So, I asked a new question, "How long do I have to make an impact?" Then our discussion suddenly shifted. The executive leaned across the table and told me I had nine months and then outlined what would happen if the business didn't have success at the end of those nine months. Wow. That was very specific. And not very achievable. Nine months was not long enough to make the trusted, thoughtful decisions that were required. Just three months prior, this same executive had told me, "Just get to know people for the first year and build relationships. Nothing else."

I admitted to myself, again, that I had definitely made a mistake. It was my fault. I didn't do the due diligence that I always counseled my friends and associates to complete. I was too comfortable that I could "work through it." That was a poor—arrogant—way to assess an opportunity. There was nobody to blame but me for this decision. There was only one path, and that was forward.

I spent the next months driving hard. Not because I was worried about my job security, but because if the business was going to have the success they wanted, change was necessary. It was the right strategic move. Six months through my tenure, I called a trusted advisor at another firm. This person was a very senior, successful, and proven executive. I asked him, "How hard do you push for change when it's needed and recognized? Even when people don't want it because they are worried about how it will impact their departments, team size, or job?" I knew I was in a tough spot. I was making sensitive decisions that were impacting lives, and there were very real office politics in play. If I wanted to "play nice in the sandbox" with other executives and build relationships, I would have to slow down on the changes I was pushing. I felt in my gut that a decision like that would not be good for the business. I needed perspective. And I got it.

My friend didn't hesitate when he answered me. He said something to the gist of, "If it's the right thing? As hard as you possibly can. Sure, if you do it, you are going to be in a tough spot, but you have nothing to lose. If you don't do it, the naysayers will come out of the shadows and say, 'I knew he couldn't do it.' You can't win. Make the changes. Be you."

Eight months after I began the role, a new leadership change was announced. My role and its headquarters were relocated to Manhattan, and the position I thought I had been prepping to step into was given to someone else. Now what? The proposed local commute—a key factor in my decision—had never materialized. Originally, I was only supposed to be in New York City maybe once a week, but that had quickly changed to commuting to New York City four to five times a week. Now, Princeton HQ wasn't even really in the picture. What was left to keep me here? Additionally, while I was asked to help build the architecture of the business unit and help the newly appointed executive succeed, every time I disagreed with a point or decision in an executive meeting, the subtle undercurrent was, "Lee is just mad he didn't get the job." That mentality wasn't going to help me or the business. I couldn't be effective with this guardrail and started to fully appreciate that my heart just wasn't in this job.

I started to realize that I wasn't even sure I wanted to be doing this kind of work anymore. I had gotten into finance to please my father. I had stayed over the years to support my family. Did I even like it? I had been doing this for more than twenty-five years. I did it well and I understood how this playbook got executed. My dissatisfaction wasn't about my abilities, my compensation, or anything related—I just wasn't happy with who I was and what I was doing. I had spent the last twenty years living for everyone else—living up to their expectations versus defining my own. I had lost much of my spirit and the soul of who I am.

After another six to eight months of going through the motions and delivering on what needed to be done, I went to my new boss and laid out the facts over dinner. I didn't want to be there anymore and, if he was honest, he didn't really want me there anymore either. We agreed that I would exit the firm. It felt good. Let's save the specifics, they don't matter in the long run. Again, I was required to fulfill a waiting period before taking another job. This time, it was eight months. Suddenly, I had the gift of time to start answering those questions that had been popping up. Where was my center? What actually brought me happiness? What did I want out of life?

The timing was good for me. It was June and the first thing I did was pack up my boys and I and go away for the whole summer. I was already raising my kids as a single parent and thought I knew them inside and out. But that summer was a revelation. With the luxury of time and focus, I noticed details I had never seen before. You think raising three boys is rinse, wash, repeat. How different could they be? Pretty damn different. Each of them has his own way about him—how he internalizes information, how he makes friends, when he has the most energy during the day, when and what he likes to eat, what time he wakes up, how sensitive he is—the list goes on. Suddenly, I was paying attention to my kids in a whole new way and learning about them in a different light. That summer was a gift to me as a father.

Don't get me wrong, it was not magic twenty-four hours a day. I still had to break up fights, regulate screen time, and ponder why kids couldn't sit down together for a meal where we all ate the same food. I had nights where I stared at the ceiling and asked myself, "What the fuck have I just done? What am I going to do now?" I had no plan. I hadn't been without a plan since I was probably twelve years old. It was scary. But I felt I was on the right path and I was starting to learn more about what I believed in and what I wanted.

As the boys got ready to go back to school in the fall, I shifted my attention to the details of my experiences. One of my moments of clarity came to me on a September day on the golf course. I'd taken up golf when I started at my first financial services company. I hadn't played much in the last several years, but I pulled my bag out thinking I would play some rounds with the new time I had. I hit the ball, and as I watched to see where it landed, I thought, "This isn't how I want to use my time." I wasn't really interested in where the ball landed. I realized golf had just been another prop in the life I had built for myself. And if I had lied to myself about that, what else had I lied about?

I started to really reflect on who I was as a person. Just as I had learned to pay attention to the details of my boys, I started to think about the details of me. What did I love to do? What games and sports did I actually enjoy? Some of the answers came quickly. I loved to surf. Why didn't I spend more time on that? I had a deep desire to hike and travel to places I had never been. What was I waiting for? More questions began to swirl in my head. What do I want to do? Where do I want to work? What is "enough"— enough money, enough success, enough time with my kids? How do I evaluate my budget in terms of what I need to make versus what I can make? Some decisions came quickly and easily. I sold the summer home. I didn't need it. I had three cars, nothing unique, but I couldn't remember why I had three. I sold two of them. I needed to simplify to get down to a foundation that I felt was rational and to get back to what mattered to me. Then I would decide what came next.

As I simplified, I realized that I could not effectively decide on the next phase of my life where I was. I needed to change my environment. I wanted to get out and think. I started planning the trip that would change the way I looked at life in total. I wanted to go someplace to learn. I wanted to surf, to hike trails, to see a different part of the world and learn more about who I was. I started cashing in airline points and favors to make it happen.

Dear Cole, Will, and Jake,

Sometimes you start down a path you think is right, only to discover months or years later that you're not headed where you want to go. Maybe you've simply lost sight of your original goals, or maybe your desired destination has changed. Whatever the case, and no matter how far you've gone, it's never too late to forge a new trail.

I love you,

Dad

LESSON #8

GET OUTSIDE YOUR COMFORT ZONE

Take a breath. Dive. I look under the water to understand why I am not moving towards shore. The leash of my board is caught on the reef and I'm stuck inside the wave. My board is banging into me and the reef is just behind me. The leash is the only thing keeping me from crashing into the reef. I know how sharp the reef is, I already have several cuts on my feet from the last ten days. If I go spinning into it, my skin will be shredded. I try to hold my breath and wait out the set of waves. It seems endless. I try to reach the reef and untangle my leash, but the waves keep breaking on me, pushing me back.

I have three options. I can release the leash and risk being forcefully pushed into the reef. I can count the waves and the seconds between, timing my breaths with the cadence, and hope I can wait it out. Or I can drown. Option two sounds best.

My mind dials up a random fact I learned just a few hours earlier from a diver from Hong Kong. The human body can exist for another sixty seconds after convulsions when gasping for air underwater. I have at least another minute for someone to get to me. Though, to be honest, does that seem likely? I'm surfing in the Indian Ocean off the Maldives and swam in from a float plane. Getting to me will not be easy as I'm caught on the "inside." I start counting waves.

A flash of memory hits me. When I was very young, I used to bob all alone in the water and count how many waves I could do before exhaustion. I know the average set at this reef is seven waves. I am at ten and the last swell was big, adding pressure that compressed me further down on the reef. Eleven, twelve, thirteen. *This has to be the last one...*

Four months prior to this trip, I had left my job and spent time with my kids. I was just awakening to the idea of focusing on what I wanted to do instead of living for everyone else. This trip was about getting out of my normal space and seeing the world through different lenses. I didn't want to tour, or sightsee. I wanted to experience. I wanted to get out of my comfort zone and accomplish something interesting.

When I decided I was going to travel, I took out a map and laid it across my desk, looking at the world. I asked myself what mattered to me and where I could go that would make me think about the world differently.

I was intrigued by India, the Indian Ocean, Southwest Asia. I had never really spent any time there. I'd taken business trips to India, but they did not usually immerse me in local culture. I had also always said I wanted to hike something. Mount Everest was a whole different kind of journey, so something like that was out. I wanted this trip to be thoughtful, spiritual.

Some of my decisions were easy. For instance, I had always been curious about Tibet. The area fascinated me. I wanted to learn meditation and understand the local perspective. I had a hunch that Tibet would leave an impression on me if I ever got there. Maybe it was time to find out? I also knew I had no interest in being in a group with hundreds of other people on some kind of trail. I was looking for unique. Why not the Forbidden Trails in Tibet?

I also wanted to surf the Indian Ocean. Everyone says to go to Bali, but a friend advised me that if I really wanted to surf open reefs and go someplace people don't know about it, I should experience the Maldives. Why not?

To complete the trip I designed, I needed permits, tour

guides, transportation, and more. Luckily, I had friends around the world who ranged from "influential" to ex-military. I also had a friend who was the general manager at a luxury hotel, and he set me up with a company that managed surf excursions around the world. With their help, I built an itinerary: New York, Dubai, Kathmandu, New Delhi, Maldives. Ocean.

Two days before I left, I sat down and became a devil's advocate. I listed every single reason I shouldn't leave. I was leaving my sons, I would be off the radar, I wouldn't be able to use my cell phone, I would be at crazy altitudes of 15,000 to 19,000 feet and had no idea if my body could handle it anymore. (My previous adventures at high altitude will be explained in the next book.) Also surfing the reefs in the Indian Ocean was dangerous. What if something happened? How would my boys even learn about it if something happened to me? There were so many reasons not to go, and I was on the verge of cancelling the whole thing. But there was a constant voice saying, "Why not?"

I stayed for Halloween, so I could trick or treat with my boys and then I left. I cashed in points and flew on Emirates to Dubai to make my connection to Kathmandu. I had never flown that airline before, and it was amazing. A stand-up bar in the middle of the plane? Seriously? What's the point of seatbelts again?

Landing in Kathmandu was a revelation. I was in a totally new world, obviously not a local. I met my guide, Jeg, who had been briefed by friends on what I was trying to accomplish, and he reviewed the rules and regulations with me. He made it very clear that his rules were about life and death. None of us knew how I was going to handle the altitude, so he also introduced me to our Sherpa, who in theory would carry the bags. We were off and running.

It was just the three of us in wooden huts, no heat, no electricity, no bathrooms. On day two, I started to question what I was doing there. On day three, Jeg suggested I stop taking pictures "If you are taking pictures, you are not fully appreciating the world you are in, the moment, and the senses. You are trying to capture a sense of it on the phone. Do what you want, but I suggest putting the phone away and being here completely."

I was never going to be here again; didn't I want photos? Didn't I want to document the experience so I could remember it and share it? But I had come on this trip to learn from other cultures. I put my phone away and tuned in to where I was completely. I was awed by the sincerity and beauty of Tibet. I never felt more connected to my surroundings. I learned that, for me, it really was better to stay in the moment and be aware enough that I could describe it after as opposed to just sharing a photo. It was a lesson I still carry with me today.

The best part of the hike was something I wouldn't have been able to accurately capture with my phone anyway: the evening sky. No light pollution. It was beautiful. Peaceful. I often thought of my sons.

Before we started off on the trails, Jeg had directed me to buy some gifts in case we ran into locals. These are long-standing rebels who judge whether or not you are permitted to pass on the trails. I'd bought some simple scarves for this purpose. Sure enough, as we were hiking on day five, three men appeared on horseback. They were completely still. I have no idea if they heard us coming and were waiting, or if we surprised them as we walked up. Jeg signaled to my bag, to do what he had explained. With one hand up, never breaking eye contact, I pulled out the scarves and handed them out. Then I stepped back, with my hands out to my side. I never felt threatened. Mostly, I was worried they wouldn't let us go on, and we would have to turn back. It felt like I was in a movie. One of the men nodded and walked over with some dried meat rolled up in parchment paper. He offered some to me and I tried it. Not the greatest steak I've ever tasted, but under the circumstances, it was so good. He made a motion to the others and we walked past. I turned back to see them staring at us, watching us leave. The next time I turned back, they were gone.

I loved this idea of giving a gift for letting us explore their world. In fact, I was disappointed in myself that Jeg had to suggest it to me. As tourists, we have such a tendency to believe we can walk in and explore anything and anywhere. We should be more grateful for the opportunity. It's another reminder I took out of the trek with me.

One night I did get very sick. At first, I thought it was the food, but in hindsight it was probably the altitude. I sat and talked with Jeg and the Sherpa. I couldn't understand half of the shit they said, and they couldn't understand half of what I said. But it all made sense. We were there to protect each other and make sure we all got home safe and alive.

Jeg did speak decent English. That night, he explained to me that the Sherpa wasn't really there to carry the stuff. He was there in case I got into an extreme situation, as Jeg would not be able to drag me out alone. He would need help. He reminded me that we were in a restricted zone by approval. "I don't know how you got these passes, but you did. But no one is going to be here to help us, unless you have someone else to call and pull more strings." It was a sobering conversation.

To get from Kathmandu to India, I had called in another favor. I met up with two guys who had an old, gutted-out, Russian military cargo plane. There was a half-drunk bottle of Yukon Jack under the pilot seat, which was one of only two seats on the plane. I sat on a bench, my back against the plane's side, a military harness keeping me secure. The pilot and co-pilot spoke Russian and broken English. They informed me that my flight was no charge, because they owed it to my friend. They argued and bitched the whole way. With every air pocket, I felt the reverberations of the plane and I thought, "This is it. This is where it all ends." I was a lifetime away from that first-class flight in on Emirates. Eventually, we landed, and let's just say it was not a smooth commercial flight landing. But I made it and I was met by an airport attendant who introduced me to my local guide. He told me to call him Swami and laughed a lot. He reminded me of Chris Berman on ESPN. I waved to the Russians and never looked back. They were still cursing at each other.

Swami took me to local communities in India where I was reminded again and again how good we have it in the United States. The extremes were striking. The smartest students were propelled to the top, but if you were deemed "less than," it seemed as if the world forgot you existed. Kids kept asking me for a dollar, begging me for a look. I was struck by how the world needs to do so much better than this. The world is not what we all think it is in our bubble. It is more. Business dinners from my past replayed in my head, times when the bill was $10,000 and plates of food went untouched. How many people could we have fed with that money instead? I thanked Swami for showing me his reality and for his brilliance in balancing pride and regret as he did so.

When I left India, I took a commercial flight to the Maldives. I was probably the only single guy on the plane. I had on my bucket hat, surf hoodie, board shorts and flip flops. I had grown a small beard and probably looked like I was from *National Geographic*. But I was never going to pass for a local. My eyes would always give it away.

My eyes, inherited from my mom, are blue. Really blue. I've gotten used to comments over the years. An optometrist even stopped me on the street once to say he had never seen eyes that shade of blue in his forty years of practice. With my dark tan, my eyes were even more noticeable, and in this part of the world, they were very different. People would grab me and put their hands on the side of my face to look at me. They would call friends and family over and point to my eyes. It happened over and over and over again. It was startling and humbling. I had no idea how to react. I blushed often.

In the Maldives, everyone was confused that I was alone. I was at honeymoon ground zero and I had no one with me. I spent ten minutes politely explaining as much to the guy who picked me up. No, we were not waiting for my wife. No, we were not waiting for my girlfriend. No, we were not waiting for my boyfriend. He simply did not believe me that I was traveling there alone. Eventually, he gave in. When I looked at the straw hut I was going to live in for the near future, I did wonder again what I was getting into. I reminded myself that my friend from the luxury hotel had set me up with a room for the end of the trip. Eventually, I would get to take a real shower. For now, it was time to surf.

I was here to be present and to surf two local breaks called Ninja and Sultans (names that don't give off an aura of safety). These were great waves, six- to eight-footers, which means if you were looking at them from the shore, they'd be twelve-plus feet high. They were beautiful, movie-like waves. The water was so clear you could look down and see the fish and coral. The local guides were all from South Africa and Australia. Just pure fun.

When it was time to find other paths after a few days, we took a float plane out to the surf. As we approached, I flashed back to prepping for the trip. I'd been told I had to be able to swim three hundred yards in current, comfortably. Leading up to the trip, I had conditioned, going to a local pool three times a week and swimming laps to build up endurance. Suddenly, it was clear why I'd been told to prepare. The break was two football fields away from where the plane settled. The only way in was to jump in with our boards and paddle in. Then I would surf the waves and paddle back. When I was counting the waves after reaching the break, one of the thoughts that floated through my head was "Fuck. Where even is the float plane?"

*This has to be the last one...*I'd been underwater for some time now—thirteen waves long—and my lungs were burning.

Luckily, that thirteenth wave was the last one. I was immediately relieved. I suddenly could move forward and out to sea a little bit more. I dove down and unwrapped my leash from the coral. As I glided on my board across the crystal-clear water, I could see the reef underneath me. It was beautiful. Minutes ago, it had been close to tearing me apart, but now it was peaceful. I started paddling back to the plane. I was exhausted. Getting caught on the inside was physically and emotionally draining. It dawned on me that thirteen waves was a really long set. Counting had made me calmer and helped me to rationally think about how to navigate the waves. It translated to a bigger lesson in my life. When you pause, think, and take time to assess your surroundings, you can pretty much get through anything. In that moment, I was reminded what I was capable of.

That experience of paddling back to the float plane was a special moment in time. I looked around at the beautiful waves and the bright colors of the fish, not a cloud in the sky. It was like surfing in an aquarium. It was gorgeous, stunning. My thought was, "Well, if I can do that, I can do anything." So then I asked myself, "What do I really want to do? What excites me the most?" I felt completely relaxed in the moment. I knew I could accomplish whatever I wanted to do. Anything was possible. If you take your time, breathe, fight through the difficult times, and if you really want it for you and not for everyone else, you can do it.

When the surf trip was done and I was ensconced in the luxury hotel, I had a drink with my guides on the porch. The sea was like glass and one of them told me it was only like that two times a year, for a week or two between winter and summer, and right now, in late November between seasons. Usually around that time there is also a lot of rain, but I'd had nothing but sun every day I had been there. The guide looked at me and smiled.

"It's almost a miracle that you can look at the water this calm. It is your spirit giving it to you."

My last weeks there, I started practicing yoga and meditating. I felt amazing. My whole world was coming together, and in two days I would get back to my kids. I was right to take the trip. I needed to get out of my surroundings, the trappings of my everyday life, unattached to technology, to get to know myself. I started a whole new path of what I wanted to do.

When I came back, I heard the same thing over and over. "You seem so happy! You look so relaxed!"

I was. And for the first time, I really felt in charge of my own life.

Dear Cole, Will, and Jake,

Travel to places you don't always feel comfortable in. Elicit the experience. Take in the moment clearly instead of through other mediums like a phone. Be present. If you listen closely enough to yourself, you'll learn what is important.

If someone invites you to experience something new, think about showing appreciation beforehand.

Always plan ahead. When things don't go to plan, know that you can get out of anything if you pause, think, and seek to understand. You have more resilience than you give yourself credit for.

Nothing is by accident. Do not depend on anyone else's perspective. When I got back from my trip, I knew the rest of my life was just beginning, and I was really excited about that. There is nothing more calming than knowing who you are and what you want to accomplish.

I love you,

Dad

LESSON #9

TAKE RISKS

It's three o'clock in the morning and I am wide awake. I stare at the ceiling as questions circle through my mind again and again. What the fuck am I doing? What about health insurance? Was this the right decision for the boys? Am I making everything harder? For what?

It's four o'clock in the morning. Different night, same questions.

Now it's two o'clock in the morning on yet another night. Same worries. Same doubts.

One night blurs into the next, but the questions never blur. They remain sharp edged and cutting.

Really, what was I thinking?

In the months following my return from my trip, new job prospects evolved easily. Many opportunities were presented to me. People I hadn't heard from in years reached out.

"Get in touch with this person, Lee, you're exactly what they're looking for."

"This job is the perfect next step for you."

"Your kind of leadership is just what this company needs."

It was flattering. These were high-paying jobs with impressive titles. Most inquiries were from well-established companies that operated in a familiar environment. I knew the playbooks well. I went on interviews. I listened. I answered questions. In some cases, I chose not to engage because I didn't want to waste their time. In the conversations I did have, I listened to what they believed was needed, I spoke about what I could bring to the table, and I gave my opinions on what direction they should go in.

But all the while I realized everything I was saying was superficial. There was a larger voice inside, coming from my soul or whatever you are comfortable calling it, questioning if this was a good move. Still, the offers came in—broad packages doing what I had successfully been doing for more than twenty years. The offers came with benefits, ensured cash flow that would deliver everything the kids needed for the foreseeable future, and an opportunity to build a larger retirement nest egg. They came with safety and comfort. I had it set. I was fortunate. Except...

Except, well, I had already proven I could do this, and I wanted to learn new skills inside segments of my industry that intrigued me. I didn't feel I needed to prove anything to anyone else anymore.

From all the conversations, the one that intrigued me the most was the offer to partner with two entrepreneurs and build a business from scratch. That's the offer I eventually took, and the one that kept me up so many nights beating myself up and questioning if I had just made a huge mistake. I realized I had never worked for me; I had worked for the perception of who I was and to provide opportunities for my children that I never had. This decision felt different. Selfish. Better.

When I was considering joining this startup, the business foundation was already set but barely off the ground. The intent, however, was there. They had an interesting business and were going to compete with finance industry leaders globally. I loved the model and the integrity with which it was thought through. I was faced with a decision. In all my previous finance roles I had been backed by exceptional brands and it sort of begged the question—

was I as good as I thought I was, or had I just benefited from being in the right place at the right time with a really strong brand behind me? I always knew that when I left those brands the companies would still succeed. I was only one person. So how much of it was actually my contribution? I knew I was not the only reason for their success, as it took many people to succeed. This new opportunity, though, was a way to find out the extent of my impact.

But could I really do this? Could I partner up with others and create something differentiated and successful? I really liked the team. I respected them. Trust had to be earned, it was not given, I've learned that, but that cuts both ways. They had integrity and credibility, but it was just us. Every decision mattered. Every relationship mattered. How would we manage to succeed when so many businesses fail? Even with all those questions unanswered after several months of consulting, I threw myself in, although I did question if my pedigree and skills were aligned with each partner's interest over the long term.

One of the turning points in my decision came when I tried to imagine *not* taking the role. When I was on my death bed and looking back at my life, did I want to know I had helped build something from scratch? I've discovered that being an entrepreneur is a gratifying, terrifying, exhilarating, and humbling adventure. I had suspected as much at the time, but I didn't know it. The only way to truly know was to do it. I realized I really did want to know. Even if our efforts failed, which I fervently hoped they wouldn't, I wanted to have the experience in my life.

I was not taking the easy road. This path required courage. Rather than steady income and benefits that came with a certain level of security, I was choosing unpredictability. Instead of building up my nest egg, I was burning through my retirement savings to pay bills. I realized almost immediately that the sacrifices my sons and I would need to make were greater than I had originally anticipated, which led to some very important and enlightening conversations with my sons.

We needed to pay attention to our budget in a way that, frankly, I hadn't done as religiously as I should have in many years. We talked about expenditures and what was really necessary. I reminded myself that a budget can be pretty simple when you are intensely focused on what truly, sincerely matters. It was also a good gut check. There were certain trips we had traditionally taken each year that I was having regrets about taking off the list, but I knew it was the right decision. When I brought it up with my boys, it turned out they didn't really care about those trips anymore. We had done them, and they were grateful and enjoyed the memories, but they didn't feel the need to go again. I was reminded, both at home and at work, of how important it is to ask questions and really listen to the answers. It was critical at home, because my boys and I had to make decisions together. It was critical at work, because if my partners and I were not on the same page, our relationship would be strained.

I knew what I was signing up for was challenging, but it was even more challenging than I expected. In a large company, there are multiple revenue streams. If one part of the business isn't working, another part of the business can cover the loss. That model can also cover a lot of mistakes. In a small business, particularly when the product you are selling is your expertise, there are no such safety nets. We were only one bad decision away from collapsing. However, we truly believed we could deliver what we said, in a differentiated way, and make a positive impact for our stakeholders. That was the fuel that kept us going. Because it certainly wasn't the perks.

The differences between my former working life and this one was striking. In past roles, if we were in a meeting and decided an idea was worth pursuing, I would delegate it to one of my many direct reports. That person would then, in turn, lead a team of people to deliver the project. Now? If we had an idea, it was my job to run with it. Previously, I had an assistant dedicated to making my life run smoothly. She managed calendar requests, booked all my travel, answered my phone. Now? I did all of that from my cell phone. I had gone from having access to the private corporate jet to booking a coach seat on the Priceline app in between answering group texts to get my kids into hockey carpools. Back in the day, if I wanted lunch, I stopped by the executive dining room. Now, if I even had time, I ran to the corner and bought a sandwich at the local bodega. Our offices were not the luxurious and sleek ones I had gone to in the past. They were pretty spartan with furniture we bought ourselves. We were not living large. We were scratching by.

The work was exhilarating. It was pared down to our ideas and who we were as people. CEOs were either going to like what we had to say and trust us, or they weren't. All the clichés like, "Say what you mean and mean what you say" proved completely true.

One of the surprises we had as we went on this journey was our own opportunities for improvement. Each of us had come from very senior roles at larger firms. When you've reached levels like that, there is an underlying assumption that you have hit expert level, and there is not a tremendous amount of development needed. Wrong. While I was very capable, without all the trappings of an established brand behind me, I realized how much I could still do to simplify my perspectives and clearly communicate with my colleagues and clients. That was also exhilarating. It was refreshing to be focused on learning and doing better every day. It was hard, but we were starting to have success.

I remember the first deal we completed. We were so excited. But in the middle of our celebration and congratulations, we were struck with a realization that we were still only one bad decision away from collapsing. Yes, we were proud of the deal, but we weren't even profitable yet. One deal is not a business. We needed to put together a lot more successes, a string of deals, to make it an enduring model that would put us on the map (or even near the map). It was humbling. That might sound depressing, but it wasn't. We were still excited, but it was an important moment in understanding what still had to be done.

Time has gone by since I joined and sold my equity in this start-up. I am both pleased and proud of what has been done. I am also aware of how different the corporate and entrepreneur paths are. I spent years of my life in meetings that were a total waste of time. When all the bureaucracy was stripped away, I realized how efficient a business can be. Don't get me wrong, big companies can be great. In my time at larger corporations, I enjoyed the work and the people. There is a lot to be said for working in that environment. But anyone who has spent time in one will tell you that there is also a lot of bureaucracy that comes with the role. There is a tremendous amount of energy spent on building empires versus focusing on the client. Stripping it all away in a small company is both scary and energizing, because you can focus on what really needs to be done. Building a thriving business is rather simple. Stay focused on what your client/market wants, deliver it, and continuously ask questions to improve. Simple.

For me, the decision to join a startup was invigorating. It was the right decision at that time. It provided me with new skills and different perspectives, and it taught me that I still have so much to learn.

Dear Cole, Will, and Jake,

Life is going to throw a lot of different turns and paths at you. No one, single path is right. Do what is right in the moment, even if it is completely different than what you have done before. Push yourself out of your comfort zone. Remember, people told Jeff Bezos his idea was ridiculous. Steve Jobs started in a garage with some people who thought he was crazy and miserable to work with. Take some risks and follow a few simple rules:

Put your best foot forward.

Align yourself with people you trust.

Don't spend more than you make.

Give it time.

Make some luck.

If you do all those things, you'll be able to overcome any problems that come your way.

I love you,

Dad

LESSON #10

APPRECIATE YOUR FRIENDSHIPS

I am sitting at a restaurant in Positano, Italy, with eight of my dearest friends, looking out over the Mediterranean Sea. Everything about the ambiance is stunning—the restaurant, the view, the fact that we are all in tuxedos and gowns. It is a picture-perfect scene. We're celebrating my birthday and sharing perspectives about our friendship and memories over the years. I am struck by the fact that, while the setting is lovely, it is not what is making the evening special. If I was with the same people eating pizza in a dive bar with a view of the parking lot out the window, I would be having just as much fun. The restaurant doesn't matter. The tuxedos don't matter. What matters are the connections I have with these people and how meaningful those are to me in my life.

Roughly a year before the Italy trip, I realized I hadn't really celebrated my birthday in about a decade, maybe two decades. I always put my birthday second to whatever other holiday or event seemed more critical at the time. It was contrary to the way I treated other people's birthdays. I always celebrated those and wanted them to feel so very special—it was their day! The day to say, "Wow, you are here and in my life, and that's amazing." I wasn't doing that for me. I was treating my birthday as more of an obligation.

I decided to plan a trip to somewhere I had never been but had always wanted to go. This would be a trip for me, as the boys were going to stay home with their mom while school was still in session. I floated the idea out to some friends, essentially saying, "Here's what I'm doing— would you like to join me?" I did not ask a huge crowd of people. While I didn't want to be exclusionary, I did not want to invite anyone who would obviously have to say no because of distance, family obligations, financial concerns, etc. I didn't want to make anyone uncomfortable. I was thoughtful with my invites, but I had no idea who would be able to make it. I mentioned it to some folks and said first come, first served. We were staying at a villa, so once I hit the number the villa could hold, we had our group.

Leading up to the trip, several of my friends reached out with the same concern. While many of them were traveling as couples, they were acutely aware that they had never met the other people on the trip. I was the only common thread. What if there was friction? What if it was uncomfortable? What if mixing all these friends from different parts of my life was like trying to mix oil and water? I understood why they were concerned, but I, oddly, was not concerned at all. I knew everyone on this trip had the important things in common—they were grounded, thoughtful, and curious. They were good people. I wasn't worried. It's funny, it was one of those things where people I fully expected to jump on it did not, and people I never expected to say yes said yes right away (people will surprise you on any given day). It ended up being the perfect mix.

It was the trip of a lifetime with a focus on experiencing the local culture. On our first day, we walked through Rome and the Colosseum. That evening, we dined at a local restaurant. I asked for silverware when we were seated, and the waitress scolded me in Italian wondering why I needed utensils when I had not ordered food yet!

The next morning, we toured the Vatican. One of my friends on the trip had arranged for a private tour given by the wife of the Pope's personal bodyguard. Due to jet lag and a late night dinner, we'd gotten only four hours of sleep, maybe. It was still a truly spectacular experience. We saw the Vatican from a perspective few people are ever privileged enough to see. It was a humbling gift, particularly coming at a time when I was questioning my faith and Christianity in general. There were moments when I had chills and that wasn't including when we walked across the Vatican grass, an absolute no-no.

We spent the next eight or nine days on the Amalfi Coast, touring Pompeii and other local sites. The beauty was beyond words. Our focus was trying to experience Italy as locals. We completed the Walk of the Gods and took a fishing boat to a small restaurant outside of Amalfi. It was breathtaking.

As a group, we laughed, ate meals, talked, drank wine, and laughed some more. I could not have predicted how quickly everyone would coalesce into one group of friends. Not only did everyone get along, they truly enjoyed each other's company, saying they felt like they had known each other for twenty years. Since that trip, as a matter of fact, there have been group chats, other vacations, and coordinated visits among different friends who met in Italy. I realized it's not the first time I've made connections like that, serving as a conduit to different groups of friends.

I had never planned a vacation before for just friends. Growing up, vacations were family affairs. As a young adult, there was no money or time for vacations. And as an adult with kids, vacations were either about family, creating experiences for my boys that they would always remember, or about solo trips for sports—skiing, surfing, etc. I had never before picked a place to experience with friends. It is a very different dynamic. On previous trips, there had always been a little something missing, even though I didn't realize it at the time. It was the sharing. While the locations were nothing short of amazing, the point of this trip was sharing it with my friends and experiencing it together.

Seeing Italy through the eyes of my friends was twice as impactful as seeing it through my eyes alone. Along the way, we shared stories and influenced each other's perspectives. They gave me the gift of telling me how I had changed their perspectives. Why aren't our goals designed around our friendships and relationships? That is what really matters. Friends matter. Relationships matter. Being connected matters.

How do you weigh those parts of your life? For me, I knew friendships were important, but I don't think I fully appreciated the value and the impact they had had on me over time. It takes energy to build a friendship and even more energy to maintain it over time.

I realized on that trip that, as often happens, one of my greatest strengths was also one of my greatest weaknesses. I have always been praised for my curiosity and for my thoughtful questions. I am generally interested when people talk to me, and because of that, I tend to ask question after question, drawing out more and more information. What I've come to realize, however, is that I was also using that skill to deflect attention from myself. I was hoarding all my thoughts and emotions, calling myself "a private person" and turning questions back around to the other person. The truth is, I just didn't want to be vulnerable. Call it my own insecurity. What happened was me limiting my experience, because I wasn't bringing the same level of transparency to the table that I was asking from others. I wasn't being authentic or present with my friends.

One memorable moment on the trip came from a day when the men and women decided to split up for a while. The men chose to take a walk and stumbled across a group of older gentlemen playing Bocce ball. We watched for a few minutes and could tell that this was a close-knit group of friends who had likely known each other for years, if not a lifetime. We struck up a conversation. While their English was not perfect, it was easy enough to communicate.

They were interested in learning about our group. Why were we there? Where were we from? Of course, we were all from different parts of the world, and they loved that. One of the older gentlemen was this five-foot-tall, impeccably dressed man (actually every man in Italy was always impeccably dressed, taking obvious pride in their appearance whether they were driving a cab, playing a game, or going to dinner—it was striking). He observed, "Ahhh. Together for a birthday. That is how it should be. You value your friend and celebrate him."

During the course of conversation, the group of men shared that they come together and play Bocce every day, prompting one of my friends to joke, "Are you married? How do you get away with that?" The men laughed, but they took the question seriously and told us about the cadence of their day. They would wake up and start the day with their wives, reading the paper, talking, sharing coffee. At some point, their wives went off and the men met to play Bocce. At the end of the day, they would meet up with their wives, have a glass of wine, prepare dinner together, eat, then maybe take a walk, and have a nightcap. The key to all of it was always being present. When they were with their wives, they were completely in the moment. When they were with their friends, they were completely with their friends. The message was clear: Be present where you are. "I love my friends as much as I love my wife," observed one man. The others laughed and poked fun at him, but I saw affection and pride in their faces. It was a simple but elegant life lesson—your friendships and your relationship with your significant other can matter equally, and when you are with them, *be* with them.

Dear Cole, Will, and Jake,

Experiences matter more than possessions, and shared experiences are the best ones of all.

Building and maintaining relationships takes energy. Try to give back twice as much as your friends give to you. You must be there to listen and to earn the right for your friends to spend time listening to you. When a friend reaches out to you, he or she is rarely asking for you to solve the problem. Ninety-nine percent of the time, what your friends need is for you to listen. Be present in their lives to what is making them stressed, sad, angry, or happy. Experience it with them. If you do those things, you will have achieved more than most people.

The trick, of course, with having high-quality friendships is letting people into your life. For real. That took me years to understand, and I sincerely hope it doesn't take you that long! While I always say listen more than you talk, and I stand by that advice, it doesn't mean you shouldn't take your turn to talk, too. If you have earned the right to talk by being a good friend or a good partner, then take it. Share what you are thinking and what you are feeling. Your life will be richer for it.

Friendships deserve great value. Treat them as such.

I love you,

Dad

LESSON #11

REMEMBER YOUR MORTALITY

I'm in a hospital room after having just completed the first colonoscopy of my life. It's a routine procedure, and for years doctors have been recommending people get their first one at age fifty. My doctor, however, said recent research indicated it's better to get it done in your forties. So here I am. I'm finished now, already changed into my clothes and just waiting for the OK to check out.

When my doctor returns, there are four other people with him. My senses become more aware. Well, as aware as they can be while still in the fog of coming out of general anesthesia.

"I want to go through your exam," says my doctor.

But I am suspicious. "Doc, I see four other people in this

room that I've never seen before. Why do I have a feeling there is more to this conversation than you telling me you will see me again in ten years?"

My doctor half smiles. The other four watch him closely for his reaction.

"We found something that causes a further discussion. There is a nodule. In simple terms, we found a tumor."

I always thought I knew how I would react if I was told I had a life-threatening illness. You see it on TV, in movies, read about it in books, and can't quite help but think to yourself, "That's not what I would do," or, "I know exactly how I would handle it." While most of us go through our day-to-day lives ignoring the fact that we are mortal, the fact is, you only have so many days in your life. Despite what we all think when we are young, we are not immortal. Not any of us. The old saying is true—the only things guaranteed are taxes and death. And, frankly, I've seen plenty of people get around taxes. I've never seen anyone get around death, though.

I was completely unprepared to hear the word *tumor*. So unprepared, in fact, I didn't even have anyone else with me at the hospital. When I made the appointment, they explained that I would not be able to drive myself home. Hospital policy was to wheel you out in a wheelchair and release you to someone, helping to put you in the car. I hated inconveniencing anyone, especially for what was just a routine procedure, but I had arranged for a friend to pick me up when I was done. When I checked in, the nurse asked if they had the right to give the person picking me up any medical information and I said no. After all, this was just a buddy giving me a ride. I hadn't told anyone I was going today. It was a routine exam. But now nothing about it was routine, and I had no one there to support me. I don't even know what the doctor said after the word *tumor*.

I know he continued to speak, because the other four with him were watching him, taking notes, looking at me, taking notes. But I don't know what was said. I defaulted to being quiet and pretending I had it under control, like I knew what they were telling me. I was in a daze. It was as if my mind had taken a snapshot of his face saying *tumor* and it was stuck in my head. I felt the doctor's hand on my arm, working to get my attention.

"Lee? Do you understand?"

I couldn't even begin to understand, but I said, "What? Yeah."

The doctor was not convinced. "It's a lot. We are going to schedule another colonoscopy. Call me tomorrow and we will go through the details. I don't think now is the right time. Everything I just told you is on this paper, in case you didn't take it all in."

With that, I put on my hat, got in the wheelchair, and was taken to my buddy downstairs. I know he helped me into the car, and I know he was cheerful and making small talk—I think about the Rangers. I was too stunned to even fake it. I just looked out the window with his voice droning in the background like Charlie Brown's teacher. When we got to my house, I thanked him, told him how much I appreciated it, and retreated into the silence of my kitchen. The boys were at school, so it was just me. I sat at the kitchen island and tried to get my thoughts together. As the shock wore off, I replayed what I could remember of the conversation with the doctor. He hadn't said I was dying. He hadn't even used the word *cancer*. I started to get my energy back.

I read all of the info, and when I called the doctor the next day, I was feeling more in control. Over the phone, he walked me through what was happening. What they found was concerning, and they wanted me to see a specialist from UPenn Hospital for another colonoscopy, ASAP, to see if she agreed with what they saw. She was an extremely busy specialist, but I was able to get on her calendar roughly three weeks later. After that colonoscopy, she confirmed that I had tumors in my appendix. She had removed some, and they had done a biopsy. I had cancer.

It was a startling thing to have my body betray me like this. I had eaten well and taken care of myself. The most frustrating thing was that I had no control over it. I couldn't fix it by changing my diet, or my workouts, or my sleep, or anything else I was in control of. I had to rely on others to solve this for me. I really hated that. I asked the specialist, "Is there anything I can do?"

"Yes, there is one thing," she said. "How you mentally approach this will matter. If you delve into the worst-case scenario, you will bring your body with it." Suddenly, in my mind's eye, I was back in that hospital bed as a college kid, paralyzed. I knew what the right mental approach could do. I had faith in myself that I could do this.

The next step was a CAT scan. The specialist felt the tumors were concentrated in the appendix but needed the test to verify. While I was on vacation visiting some friends, I got the call with the results. They needed another CAT scan. That couldn't be good. After the second round of CAT scans, they informed me that it wasn't just in the appendix. It was also in the colon. I could have surgery or chemo. My immediate reaction was similar, again, to my injury in college. "No chemo. Cut it all out," I directed.

This was in spring, and the doctors immediately started looking at surgery dates. But I wanted to enjoy the summer with my kids and told them I would do it in the fall.

"Every month you keep waiting, it could get worse," warned the doctor.

It was a balancing act. I was facing mortality and wanting, obviously, to get better as soon as possible. But I was also more aware than ever that you never get a day back, and summers with the kids are precious. I stubbornly stood my ground. After some back and forth, the doctor agreed that if I would do a colonoscopy once a month between then and surgery so they could monitor the status of the tumors, I could wait.

Let me tell you, if you ever want to keep yourself thin and eating in a simple way, agree to monthly colonoscopies for seven months!

Even when fall arrived, I kept pushing the surgery off. I was struggling with two issues. The first was fear, triggered by the memory of a friend who had passed many years before. When he felt increased pain in his abdomen, he requested a typical checkup with his doctor but ultimately was diagnosed with cancer. He proceeded to have surgery only to be told the cancer had spread beyond their ability to cure him. He learned of his illness and died within two months. I have never seen a man so full of life taken so quickly.

The second issue was more complicated. I had purchased a

significant amount of life insurance many years ago at my peak of health. I'd also set up a trust for each of the boys, which the insurance would fund in the event of my death. (Each trust includes hurdles the boys need to accomplish to receive any benefits, such as achieving a college degree, minimum age limits, limited withdrawal rationale, and demands on philanthropy to name a few.) Doing the math, my sons would receive a significant financial windfall if I passed away. The simple truth was I doubted my ability to accumulate a similar amount of money for my sons over my lifetime. I started to question what was truly important. I thought this would be an easy debate for myself, but I found my intellect weighing the benefit of liquid wealth for my sons and the freedom it would provide. Ultimately, I settled on a strong belief that no amount of money can replace a father's care, love, guidance, and listening.

I was originally hoping to delay the surgery to the first part of 2020, but I finally agreed to a date in December 2019.

The entire time, from diagnosis to just before the surgery, I kept what I was going through mostly to myself. I didn't tell my boys, I didn't tell my mom and dad, and I didn't tell most of my friends. I didn't want anyone to worry or to burden them. There was another selfish reason as well. I did tell one friend, who lived in Seattle, and that guy promptly started bugging the shit out of me. It was text after fucking text asking me when I was going to schedule the surgery. Yes, I know it was out of concern, and he's a very dear friend, but I wasn't going to open myself up to more of that from any other friends, so I shut it down and kept it to myself.

I just didn't want to be that vulnerable with others. While I was going about my life for those months, I realized how easy it was to keep conversations superficial. I deflected questions about myself back to others. I became more and more aware of how much minutia we worry about that truly doesn't matter.

"What if my kid doesn't get into the school he wants to go to?"

"I'm not making enough money."

"I don't think junior made the right team."

I don't want to belittle the concerns others discussed. Real life is made up of many moments, but perspective is a game changer.

About a week before the surgery, I told my boys. I told the older two boys, ages sixteen and fourteen, when we were in the car together. I explained that the doctors had found tumors in my appendix and colon, and they were going to remove them a week after Thanksgiving. I told them the doctors would cut everything out, and I was going to be OK. I didn't want them to be scared. They accepted that and seemed to take it in stride.

"Will you be good after that?" they asked.

I said yes, and that was the end of it. I don't think it occurred to them that the surgery could go any other way.

When I told my youngest, he had a different question. "Will you be faster after the surgery?" he asked.

I wasn't sure where he was going with that. "What do you mean?" I asked.

"Well, you seem to be getting slower. So, will you be faster again?"

Laughing, I confirmed I would be faster again and that was enough for him.

As I was waiting to go into surgery, I started to worry and wish maybe I had given them a little more insight into the potential outcomes. I wanted to protect them from the anxiety, but was that the right thing? Should I have prepared them for the other possibilities? Had I done the right thing for my boys by glossing over the risks? Being a parent and making decisions like that is never easy. I did the best I knew how to do at that moment and, luckily, it turned out fine (skipping over many details which don't add much value here). The surgery was successful, and the doctors told me they got it all. They said I should take care of myself and restart my life.

With a clean bill of health, I started reaching out to friends and family to explain what I had gone through and that I was going to be fine. [I even reached out to the pain-in-the-ass friend in Seattle and thanked him for all his pushing. I likely would have postponed the surgery longer if not for him. Thank you, but he's still a pain in the ass. ;)] Time and time again, the responses came back with sincere requests of, "What can I do for you?" And my response was the same over and over. I encouraged them to push the people in their lives to get their colonoscopies and not put it off. I wasn't looking for pity or attention when I made those calls and sent those texts. I just wanted to take some of my own advice. I knew that if my boys were in the same situation I had been in, I would counsel them to approach it differently and to let people in. These people mattered to me, and I knew I mattered to them, so I let them in. It was important to take the time and tell them what had happened and that I was going to be OK.

Now, as I write this, it's two days after the surgery. I am in tons of pain. Everything hurts. But I have a new start. The rest of my life is just beginning, and I can decide how it plays out. I have more freedom and greater clarity than I have ever had before. I want this feeling for my boys and hopefully at a much earlier stage in life.

Dear Cole, Will, and Jake,

We all have a limited number of days in this world. Some have more than others, but none of us have forever. Think about how you live those days. Build a life that you enjoy.

Living every day as fully as possible does not mean going to extremes for fun. It means being present, valuing relationships, having meaningful experiences. It means keeping perspective and understanding what a challenge truly is.

Look at the challenges in your life and try to assess them for what they are without making them mean too much. Evaluate. Prioritize. Determine what is really a problem and what is just being perceived as a problem. Often, it's a result of outside influences.

When the unpredictable comes your way, don't go it alone. Bring your friends in. Let them help you, even if they just know enough to ask, "How are you today?"

I love you,

Dad

TAKE THE TIME NOW TO AVOID REGRETS LATER

"Lee? I'm about to go in the room. I'm glad I caught you," the nurse says. "I don't know how much time he has left."

My cousin warned me, so I knew the FaceTime call was coming and I answered immediately. Still, I'm unprepared for the sight of a nurse in a full hazmat suit.

"I'm going to open the door, go in, and hold the phone to his face," the nurse continues. "You will have a chance to talk to him. It will sound muffled, distant."

She opens the door, and I can see the windowless hospital room. In the center of the room is my uncle, hooked up to tubes and IVs and wearing a mask for the ventilator/

respirator. The nurse reaches the bed and holds the phone over him. She disappears and his face suddenly fills the screen. He gives me a smile, looks me in the eye and says, "Fucking Chinese."

"Uncle Bruce, how are you? Tell me," I say.

"I don't know how much time I have left. They gave me a bunch of morphine," he says with a half-smile on his face. "I'm sorry we never got together as much as we should have. I'm sorry I didn't talk more about your mom and what she meant to me. I'm sorry that you just lost her."

The nurse angles in and reminds us both that he needs to save his strength.

"I wish someone could be there with you," I say. "I wish someone could hold your hand. I'm sorry."

"I'll play through this," he responds.

We both say I love you and then the nurse leaves the room.

She comes back on the screen without her hazmat suit for her final words. "I hope that helped you. He doesn't have much time left, so whatever the family needs to do to let others know, I would do it."

She is not unkind, but there is nothing else she can offer us. She hangs up. My uncle dies the next morning.

Five days prior to my last conversation with my uncle, my cousin sent me a text: "My dad doesn't feel that good—slow, lethargic."

My uncle, while eighty-two years old, was in perfect physical condition. He was a proud Navy veteran and military academy graduate who regularly went on fifty-mile bike rides and skied the toughest trails.

"He has a little bit of a cough and he is slow and feeling down."

I agreed with my cousin that she should get him checked out by a doctor, but this was a healthy guy living alone in Eagle, Colorado. I was not seriously thinking of COVID-19.

He went to the doctor for a checkup on a Thursday. The next day, he was feeling worse. He told his daughter he was worn down and couldn't get around. The doctor, fearing it could potentially be COVID-19, sent a special ambulance to pick him up. My cousin watched him get taken out of his townhouse and moved into the ambulance. It was the last time she saw her father in person.

Once at the hospital he was immediately quarantined.

They moved him to a wing with no windows. The hospital explained they had to manage it that way because they didn't have enough rooms to house everyone. No one was able to physically see my uncle. There was no visiting. There were no final goodbyes.

When he reached the hospital, they tested him for COVID. The next day, Saturday, they processed the test. By Sunday morning, they had the news that 90 percent of his organs were failing or had already failed.

When my cousin got the call, she asked, "How much time does he have left?" She expected them to say weeks or days, but they told her it was hours. That was the same day she called me and told me to expect a call from the nurse.

The important part of my final interaction with my uncle isn't about COVID-19 and what a serious disease it can be. It's about what was going through my uncle's mind in the final hours of his life—what he felt was most important to communicate to his loved ones. It could have just as easily been a stroke that put him in that hospital bed. What has stuck with me is that his regrets were all about relationships—the time he invested in them, the moments he missed, the things he hadn't said. Perhaps the isolation made the regrets more profound. I'll never know. But it made me reflective, once again, of what's important.

I wish my boys and I took more trips to ski with him. Sure, we did a number of these trips over the years but not consistently. Life always seemed to get in the way. He called every year with the first snow reports. I thought that would go on forever. He was my ace in the hole when I wanted to surprise skier friends. When they skied in Colorado, I would have them look up my uncle, the first ski instructor ever at Vail Mountain, so he could take them out on the slopes. These friends were excellent skiers. They would arrive, take one look at him with his Santa Claus beard, and assume they were going to be babysitting the old guy. "What was Lee thinking?" they'd wonder. Then, consistently, they would call me halfway through the day and say, "Who IS this guy? I can't keep up." It never occurred to me that the last friend I sent to him (this past winter) would be the last time I had that laugh.

When I called my cousin to check on her a week after my uncle passed, she said she was mostly feeling numb. But she, too, was regretting the times lost. She complained about the long weekends they had talked about that she had never followed up on and made happen. She always thought there would be more time.

Losing my uncle in this way was startling because of how sudden it was and because we couldn't be with him at the end. It was also startling because I had just lost my mother a month earlier.

I was so grateful to my Uncle Bruce for being present during my mom's last days. One night, we went to dinner away from the hospice and he talked to me about my mom and how much he appreciated her as a sister. He also told me how he appreciated me and how my "everything happens for a reason" approach to life had helped him over the years. He then shared some advice of his own.

He acknowledged that I hadn't actually asked for any advice, but he felt it was important to say his part. "I got divorced twenty-five-plus years ago and I always thought I would meet someone new. I got the dogs and, frankly, I got used to being alone. But growing old alone is not a lot of fun. It's really lonely. I miss being around someone. I think maybe I was looking for someone perfect—and no one is perfect," he said. He didn't outright tell me what to do, but I understood his point and appreciated his perspective. It was only a month later I lost him. I'll miss him.

That dinner took place in Syracuse, because that was where my mom chose to spend her final days. In late December, she called me and said she had gotten a call from her doctor. She had cancer and it was in her entire body.

"How did they not find it?" I demanded.

But Mom had already moved on and had a plan. "I can't change that," she told me. "They said I have about six months to a year left, and I want to move back to Syracuse and spend time with my friends."

I wanted whatever was going to make her happy. She and my dad had been living in South Carolina for ten years at that point, and his dementia was getting worse. She was the caregiver and that role needed to change. My brother and I rented them an apartment in Syracuse and moved her up right away. Unfortunately, she went downhill very quickly. It was challenging from the day she stepped off the plane. I remember sleeping on the floor in their apartment guest room on Christmas Eve, helping her transition from the bathroom and back to bed through the night. Fast forward just two weeks and we were lucky enough to find a bed in hospice. I spent my time driving back and forth to Syracuse as she slowly slipped away from me.

From that first call in December until she couldn't speak anymore, we had the gift of talking about what really mattered. I feel lucky that we had the ability to speak about so many things—what it was like to grow up, to be with her brother, what her childhood was like. By the time she passed, we'd had all the important conversations. Cancer takes away so much, but that is one thing it gives back—an opportunity to talk about things in a prepared way, a catalyst to stop procrastinating on those important conversations.

In early February, she passed. Once again, I had regrets. There were so many little events that I wish I had made the time to fly down and see her for. Maybe it was impossible. Managing work, three kids, my own health concerns, a relationship—I obviously had my hands full. But I wish I had doubled my efforts.

After she passed, I realized I didn't really know how to grieve. I had lost other people in my life, but nothing felt like this. I was numb. Then I lost her brother. Some mornings, I would wake up crying. In my dreams, my mom was hugging me, and when I woke up, it was like losing her all over again. It was upsetting, but I put my feet down, breathed in and out, and started moving forward on the day. Small memories wove in and out. I never understood loss like that or what grief that deep would feel like.

In one dream, she told me, "I feel really alone. Can you come get me?" I woke up that morning and called my brother.

"Where is Mom's urn?" I asked. Long, quiet pause. When my mother was cremated, we had a plan for spreading the ashes, but we needed the snow to melt. Then the virus came and paused the burial. My brother remained quiet. "Where is it?" I pressed.

"It's at the funeral home," he admitted.

WTF. He had agreed to bring it home.

"Well, go get her! She feels all alone."

My brother called an hour later, assuring me he was on his way home with Mom. I was relieved. It did occur to me after my uncle passed just a month later, that when her brother joined her on the other side, my mom would be less lonely. Was that what she had been trying to tell me? That she needed someone with her? Believe what you will, but the idea that her brother was called so soon so she wouldn't be lonely gave me some comfort.

I know my mom wouldn't want me to feel lost or bad. In fact, when she knew she was going, she had a pretty specific list of what she wanted from me (that's Mom!). She had a plan for where her ashes would be spread. She felt family was important and wanted me to take care of my dad and to spend time with my brother but also cautioned me from making my boys my entire life. She had met my girlfriend and declared her "a gift" and told me to never let go of her. She reassured me that she was going to a much better place and didn't want me to worry, joking, "I don't have to listen to your father bitch anymore." Lastly, she told me to get a dog.

Mom felt strongly about the role dogs play in our lives, and she pointed out that I had been waiting a decade and she didn't want me to wait anymore. I picked up my golden retriever puppy, Bodhi, on April 20, 2020, and find his presence comforting. I feel connected to Mom through his love and am enjoying watching my own sons create a bond. Sometimes, moms really do know best.

Dear Cole, Will, and Jake,

When I go, or when someone else important in your life goes, remember the impact they have had on you and the wonderful experiences and memories you shared. More importantly, while you have those people still in your life, carve out time for them. Prioritize things you both agree are important and do them. No one is perfect, and you will not do every single thing you could. But I think I could have done better with my mom and uncle. That regret is heavy.

Prioritize at least one experience a year that you share—as small or as large as you want. You really don't know how much people matter until they're gone.

Death is not something you can avoid. It's not the most terrible thing in the world. It is a passing. I believe there is someone a lot bigger than us who needed my mom more than we did at that point. They needed an angel. And then another one in my uncle. Tell your children, my grandchildren, and pass it on.

I love you,

Dad

PREPARE FOR THE NEXT WAVE

It's early morning. I am sitting down for my morning meditation. Just ten minutes to orient my life. I open my eyes when finished and look out through the bay window at my back property. I lost track of time and location and the view brings me back to the present. The sun is just rising over the tree line on this cold morning. There is an apple tree over to the right and all the leaves have already fallen. A light frost covers the trees. Just then, a brilliant red cardinal lands on a branch. It's the first time I have seen one since last winter. In Native American symbolism, the red cardinal represents the spirit and reminds you to reconnect with a relationship. I have gotten my answer on where I need to focus today.

You can relax now, the last wave is passing. Stay with me a little longer, please.

We have come a long way in a short time. I've attempted to teach you lessons that are evergreen:

- Build relationships on care and respect, not fear.
- Make your own decisions.
- Trust your gut.
- Find your inner strength.
- Understand how others see you, but don't let them define you.
- Choose your partner carefully.
- Regularly reevaluate who you are and what you want.
- Get outside your comfort zone.
- Take risks.
- Appreciate your friendships.
- Remember your mortality.
- Take the time now to avoid regrets later.

And now it is time for the final lesson: prepare for the next wave.

In life, you never know what wave, or lesson, you will face next, but you can prepare for whatever may come by fostering greater awareness—a deep understanding of yourself. Awareness is something you must seek to rediscover every day. It will increase your confidence, simplify your life, calm your mind, and allow you to control your path.

For me, the biggest learning I have had, which occurred

pretty recently, is that without awareness—until you really love yourself, respect yourself, know yourself, and understand what truly matters to you—you are always going to feel lost. You will always be searching for an external lighthouse, which isn't there.

There are a lot of ways to achieve this understanding. There are formal programs and online courses and classes you can take around the world. As I've mentioned, I don't profess to have all the answers, but I do have two recommendations for increasing your awareness.

Recommendation one: Start appreciating the four foundations of you and your life—the Body, Intellect, Emotions, and Spirit. Each foundation has a profound impact on your day-to-day life, and if you don't recognize their existence and have a path to align them, you will continuously make less-informed decisions, leading to inconsistency and unfulfilled potential.

Body. Your body is a carrier. That's all it actually is. The body is incredibly important, because it is what allows you to participate in the world, but the physical is overemphasized in our society—that's the superficial nature of our society. Personally, I've spent too much of my life worrying about how my body worked and what physical feats it could accomplish. Listen to what your body needs. Understand how to take care of it. Provide it with nutrition, wellness, and be grateful for what it allows you to do. But don't lose sight of the fact that it is just the carrier.

Intellect. Your intellect has different ranges on different days. The intellect can be a powerful ally, but it can also put you in positions you don't want to be in. Ask what it is looking for and what makes you happy, but don't let it lead you.

Emotions. The emotions are the complement to the intellect. They allow you to dance when everyone is looking, sing when you are uncomfortable, be silly, and spontaneous. How emotionally mature are you? Is your emotional maturity the same age as your physical body? Younger? Older? Like the intellect, emotions can lead you on a destructive path if not properly balanced. I can recall many instances where insecurity from my emotional state led to short-term decisions that were not productive for me or others involved—competing on the athletic field and worrying someone was superior, feeling unappreciated at work, and responding with overcommunication, trying to be one of the boys before I was one of the boys. The list goes on and on. As with the intellect, be aware of what your emotional state is and ask what it needs, but don't let it run the show.

Spirit. Lastly, most importantly, is the spiritual self. I went my entire life, until very recently, not understanding this part of me. The spirit incorporates what the body, intellect, and emotions need. It orchestrates the rest of your being and gets you to the very best place for you. The spiritual self is what should have been leading my decisions, but until recently, I didn't even know it existed. I paid no attention. I didn't inquire. I spent my life letting intellect or emotion lead me. That may have led to some short-term highs, but over the long term, the path always returned to frustration, anger, anxiety, questioning self-worth, you name it. Allow your spirit to give you advice and guidance to make thoughtful decisions about what is important so that you can love yourself, know what you want, and why.

Recommendation two: check in with all four foundations daily and before making a decision. As you have read through my life's story, you may have noticed that many decisions I made were dependent upon one or two foundations. The worst decisions I've ever made were built upon only one, typically emotions.

By taking one, five, or ten minutes to check in with how your foundations feel about any decision, you can align your interests and ascertain if this choice is best for you.

Sounds simple, right? Try it for a day, just one day. You'll find it is much harder to listen to yourself and align quickly than you expected, due to so many outside influences and "noise." I have read that the average adult attention span is eight seconds, and each day, people spend an average of ninety minutes on Snapchat and sixty minutes on Instagram. I can't recall where I read these figures, and they might be outdated at this point, but they're directionally right. It is very hard for people to focus on themselves, and I would argue that taking time to look inward is more important than ever.

With constant texts, Snapchats, thoughts about who's doing what, your practice schedule, your worries, how others may view you, parents talking at you, driving, Fortnite, etc....there is always "noise." It's important to find a quiet place for a couple minutes, close your eyes, and ask yourself, "How does my body, mind, emotions, and spirit feel about...speaking to my friend about how they hurt me, asking a spouse how she feels about our relationship, telling a teacher I don't know how to do this work and need help, asking my parent how they are doing, asking myself how I feel." The issue doesn't matter. If you take these few moments to inquire within and listen to each foundation, your life will be led by you. So start. Today. A few minutes a day will change your life. It has been scientifically proven that the practice of meditation changes the way your brain works. You will have greater conviction in your decisions. The world will seem less complex. It all begins and ends with you.

With the lessons of this book, you now know how to ride

each set of waves, which is good, because they always come. Some bigger and some smaller, but they always come. Now you have a plan in which to not only survive but to thrive.

Dear Cole, Will, and Jake,

I thought many, many times about what I should write in this last letter. I wanted to be thoughtful and brilliant. In reality, I'm just a dad from a small town who loves his three sons more than life itself.

I believe everyone has the potential to accomplish great things, and we are all on this earth for a reason. Whomever you choose to love, love them deeply. Whatever you choose to pursue for a career, pursue it with passion. Cherish the relationships you develop and treat them as an asset. Get to know yourself well from the inside, as the inside is what people actually see. Spend less than you make and make decisions that have purpose. Know that you will make many mistakes and have numerous failures and challenges. They are never a bad experience if you learn from them.

I have always been and always will be proud of you. I hope you have enjoyed this book. (I know what a pain in the ass it was trying to get you to start, continue, and finish summer reading when you were growing up... ;)

Love,

Dad

"The goal is not to be better than the other man, but your previous self."

—DALAI LAMA

ACKNOWLEDGMENTS

My sincerest gratitude to:

My sons, for the obvious inspiration.

Mom and Dad, I don't have enough space to express my appreciation for your sacrifices and love. Thank you.

Shannon, for your support. You are a gift to us, and without you, this book would never have been completed. I love you.

Sam and Will, for donating (unknowingly) your mom's time to help me and for making me laugh.

Jay, for being you. Love you, brother.

Liz, for my sons.

My uncles, for being there and showing me different paths.

All my friends, you influenced this book in some way, particularly Scott Trethewey. Thank you, all.

My publisher and the Scribe Media team, you were amazing. Special thanks to Kayla Sokol for helping me manage the project, Kelsey Adams for the heartfelt edits and confidence, and Rachel Brandenburg for her creativity and patience with my cover.

Scribe Media, (again) who treated me as if I was of great value, and I so appreciate your care with my idea.

Beth Kupchinsky, for helping me get started.

All the mentors in my life, especially my teachers in middle and high school, thank you for never giving up on me and always making the extra effort.

Lastly, thank you, Nantucket, and your locals for providing the spirit to start my writing.

If I left anyone out who was expecting to be listed here, I'm sorry. Every person in my life had a place in this book in some way. Thank you.

ABOUT THE AUTHOR

LEE D. BECK was a recruited college athlete who became an assistant professor and assistant coach before he transitioned into financial services. Lee held various executive roles at PIMCO, J.P. Morgan, and Blackrock, and has earned his BSE, MA, and MBA. A math and reading development volunteer for at-risk city school districts, Lee commits a portion of his earnings to charities focused on urban development. Lee enjoys searching for rural surf breaks to watch the ocean and enjoy the ride.

Made in the USA
Monee, IL
21 December 2020